EDUCATION THROUGH ENGLISH

EDUCATION THROUGH ENGLISH

The Use of English in African Schools

BY

EVA ENGHOLM

CAMBRIDGE
AT THE UNIVERSITY PRESS
1965

PUBLISHED BY
THE SYNDICS OF THE CAMBRIDGE UNIVERSITY PRESS
Bentley House, 200 Euston Road, London, N.W.1
American Branch: 32 East 57th Street, New York, N.Y 10022
West African Office: P.O. Box 33, Ibadan, Nigeria

Printed in Great Britain by
THE STELLAR PRESS LTD.
UNION STREET, BARNET, HERTS.

LIBRARY OF CONGRESS CATALOGUE
CARD NUMBER: 64-21543

CONTENTS

LIST OF PLATES

The Plates are bound in at the end of the volume

INTRODUCTION: A STATEMENT OF THE PROBLEM

The Nature of the Imaginative Process.

'The highest and most delicate reaches of human life depend upon an imaginative anticipation of potentialities not yet actualised.'[1]

I remember a student in England returning to College after taking a painting lesson in a junior class, and saying to me, 'You know, this class really hasn't got any imagination. None at all'. I asked what they had been painting. 'An imaginary monster', she said. She produced a set of nasty, mostly brown and black torpedo-like objects. I asked her how she had introduced the subject to the children and what she had said. It transpired that she had said nothing other than, 'I want you to paint a terrible monster—not a real one, just a monster out of your head, an imaginary one'. When I said, 'Then that's your fault, isn't it? You haven't tried to find out whether the children have any imagination', she looked injured. It is essential for the teacher to draw upon the children's stock of imagery, by the associations she calls up and by the stimulating effect of the actual words she uses in expressing her own images. Suppose I say to a class,

To-day we will paint a picture of a most fearful and terrible monster or dragon, and I want it to look so terrifying that everybody that looks at your painting will feel frightened. Now, I can think of a monster bigger than an elephant, a scaly monster, with scales as big as dinner-plates clanking on its sides. It has terrifying jaws, like the scoop on the end of a crane. Scarlet and orange-coloured smoke comes out in puffs from the huge black holes which are its nostrils, and the smoke has a revolting, suffocating smell. It has eyebrows like mops, and flashing eyes, and terrible ears like fungi. Because

[1] Cohen, *Reason and Nature*, ch. 2 (Free Press, 1953).

> it lives in the sea all sorts of shells and sea-weeds have grown on its scaly sides, all colours, crimson, like sea-anemones, and yellow and vivid green. It has a row of spikes down its back, and a fearful slimy tail, fifty yards long, which it lashes in and out of the water, and the water foams and hisses as the monster moves through the waves.

What is actually happening is that the words (and of course the tone of voice) used by the teacher evoke in each child a series of images; the images evoked are peculiar to each child, and are accompanied by his own emotional associations. By reflecting upon and using his imagery the child creates out of it an 'imaginary sea-monster'. But imagination also has 'its feet on the ground', for the images depend on sense perceptions of actual things, like dinner-plates, fire, mops, smoke, hiss of waves, smell and so forth. The teacher who fails to recognize the nature of this process may have a bleak return. This may lead him to the conclusion that his material is at fault (that is 'The children have no imagination'): in fact, it is the teacher's imagination that is at fault.

In 1953 I started teaching English as a second language, and Art in an African Secondary school (mostly boys). I found myself having to start again from the beginning, after twenty-one years of teaching and teacher training. My early classroom experiences in Africa were totally unlike any I had had previously. One is aware, of course, that one of the main devices in teaching is teaching by analogy, but just to what extent one depends on this device was not fully brought home to me till I found myself in a situation where practically none of my analogies were of any use.

Repeatedly I found myself beginning, 'Well, it's like a . . .', only to realize that the simile was unknown to my African pupils, and did not apply in Uganda anyway. But how was one to make comparisons that were meaningful?—for to teach without making comparisons is impossible, and every comparison involves an act of imagination. Added to this was the deadly bleakness of being asked no questions. For eighteen months on one ever asked a question (this was partly because of the children's lack of facility in the English language), so that the bliss of classes of children eager to learn was off-set by an apparently total lack of curiosity. One left the classroom a limp rag. There was no come-back, no stimulation, no urgent follower frantically demanding the answer to just one more question. I remember thinking ruefully of how often and with what confidence I had taught students in England that curiosity was 'natural' in children.

There was much inquisitiveness (I could never do anything without being watched), but the concepts of animism which are part of the thinking of many Africans did not seem to lead to the rigorous observation of cause and effect produced by western scientific concepts.

I once asked an African teacher, who had herself spent a considerable time in England, about this lack of questions. 'They do not know what questions to ask', she said. Questions, comparisons, all are the outcome of the ability to reflect upon imagery and association, and depend on sense experience, on awareness, on observation, and a certain degree of consciousness, and this again is largely governed by interest. You cannot ask questions about things beyond the range of your imaginative participation.

Cohen in *Reason and Nature* has summed up this situation as follows:

> We are led to the same results [that is the recognition of how images must be subordinated to rational connections] by reflecting how dependent our power of imagining things is on our previous experience .... Without reflecting, the field of unfamiliar possibilities is closed. The reader can test this for himself by asking how many people can imagine a piece of paper that does not have two distinct sides, or a vessel where there can be no line of demarcation between inside and outside. (A Mobius strip or Kummer surface)

This inability to cope with what was beyond the reach of their imagery and associations, was clearly demonstrated when the children eventually began to ask questions—simple questions about concrete things. (The questions beginning with 'How?' or 'Why?' came later.) 'Madam, what is a horse?' 'Well, a horse is about the size of a cow, but it hasn't any horns.' Unnerved by the ludicrous image, I added hastily, 'and it has a mane', only to realize that the word had no meaning for any of the pupils for they had never seen a mane. The ruff of a lion would be the nearest thing, but contrary to popular belief, relatively few children in this part of Africa have seen a lion. Of course, the obvious comment is, 'produce a picture of a horse'. But pictures themselves imply a habit of looking at pictures, a familiarity with pictures, so that the beholder can translate them into some reasonably satisfactory concept. Looking at pictures takes for granted European eye habits. In our painting lessons these habits had been disconcertingly absent. Moreover when shown film-strips, many of the things represented proved completely meaningless to some, and only vaguely comprehensible to others. 'Madam, what is snow?' 'Well, you only get it where it is very cold. You know when the rain is very cold . . .' What was one to say? Snow is like salt? (The amethyst-coloured lumps from the local salt-lakes sold in the market, most familiar to country Africans?—The packets of dirty-grey cooking-salt sold to town Africans?) No good. Snow is like sugar? (The local sugar is made from sugar-cane and greatly resembles the cooking-salt, a source of occasional culinary disaster, and anyhow how could one explain feet and feet of sugar on the African landscape, with sugar on the trees, which in Uganda do not seasonally lose their leaves?) Hopeless. And then, apart from a winter landscape, what about winter—or any season? What about ships, or the sea? The children always referred to Lake Victoria as 'the sea', but to anyone who has experienced a sea, the comparison would seem absurd, so many and profound are the differences.

What is an eiderdown? Here at least the answer was relatively easy for one can take an eiderdown (I occasionally used one) into the classroom, also a bedspread, and all the other appurtenances of a European bed. It was possible then to establish before the astonished gaze of an interested class just how complicated European sleeping arrangements are.

Even among Europeans, bed divergencies cause a certain amount of consternation, and the dismay of a pure-blooded Briton when making his first acquaintance with the German 'Federbett', for example, never mind about the Swiss or Austrian buttoned blankets, is a common phenomenon.

Nevertheless, when teaching German or French to English children it is possible to give some idea of what a German bed or even a French 'bidet' is like, because there is a common stock of imagery to draw upon, and it is possible for a teacher to arouse the necessary chain of associations. But try to explain to an African child the appearance and uses of an eiderdown, and see how soon this exercise can undermine one's confidence. (The other articles of bed-clothes, also the bed and mattress were known in varying degrees, being best known among those African children who enjoyed boarding facilities during the period of their secondary schooling.)

On the other hand it was dangerously easy to deceive oneself into thinking that one had described an unknown object efficiently because of the keen desire of the children to understand, their equally keen desire to please the teacher and their rather vague appreciation of the term 'understand'. This was partly due to a form of education which aimed in the first place at mass literacy, and where, even at the next most vital stage, the approach was quantitative. This meant that the vital imaginative step, the forming of ideas by reflecting upon the reservoir of images and associations, was omitted.

The very recognition that there is something which we have not yet grasped involves something beyond imagery. Without such recognition of our formal power to recognize the limitations of our material imagination (that is, imagery *alone*) we fall into the absurd sophistry which ignores the most patent of all facts, viz. human ignorance, and asks, 'How can we know that there is anything which we don't or can't know?' This sophistry is not only the basis of what is called subjective idealism but is the key to all that is characteristically weakest in modern thought—the illusion that by ignoring our limitations we can deny the larger world that mocks our pettiness.[1]

It is precisely this weakness which we must be careful not to encourage in the young members of a newly developing country. Our pupils in African schools, aided by excellent memories (and the laws of probability and chance) can give the impression of having grasped a situation or the meaning of a thing, when actually the very opposite turns out to be the case. It is only too easy to become glib about it all, to skate slickly on the surface, and this glibness is a menace against which the teacher in an African school has to be on his guard all the time.

It could be said that I am making too much fuss about such things. After all, in teaching European children one often has to tackle the explanation of something unknown. Unknown, yes, but never totally outside the range of the children's imagery and associations, that is, beyond their imaginative participation. The Arctic can be defined in terms of known images, so can the desert, so can a Chinese house or Chinese sleeping arrangements. There are hundreds of pictorial 'aids' readily comprehensible to European children on account of their familiarity with the medium—but try and describe Mount Everest or King Arthur and his Knights to an African child. I did take the School Certificate class to see the film of the conquest of Everest and also the film of the Kontiki Expedition. Those who had never before visited a cinema (and they were the majority) were in the first instance almost entirely preoccupied with the seats (tip-up and plush). Later, when I set the School Certificate class the question, 'Having seen the films, if you were now asked which of the two expeditions you would care to join, which would you choose?' a number wrote that they would prefer to join the Everest expedition because it was not dangerous, whereas you *could* fall

[1] Cohen, *Reason and Nature*,[2] ch. 9, 'An Essay on the meaning of scientific method'. (Free Press, 1953.)

off a raft. Others chose the Kontiki because lying on a raft in the sun seemingly doing nothing, with a lot of food about, offered understandable standards of comfort apparently absent from the Mount Everest expedition. After reading *The Lady of Shalott,* which was warmly received on account of its sounds and the 'curse', I was asked what did the Lady of Shalott eat, who brought it to her, and where were her parents and relatives? Cornered, and longing to be able to help by somehow meeting them half-way, I tentatively suggested that her father might easily have been killed in battle and perhaps her mother had died (death is a familiar occurrence and taken for granted), and then, as they knew, many Europeans did not have hordes of brothers, sisters and in-laws. But the Lady of Shalott was a lady of high degree and probably had a maidservant, a lady-in-waiting, who would bring her food. (After all, Tennyson had not written the poem with the Baganda in mind). From then on, most written questions concerning the poem began, 'The Lady of Shalott lived on an Island with her waiting-woman. Her father had been killed . . . .', because this made sense, and was within their imaginative grasp. There are islands in Lake Victoria, an African Princess could live on one; she could even live in a peculiar building, and they were willing to accept her odd isolation as a European divergence from the usual. One boy actually wrote, 'She lived on an Island in the Lake', thus showing clearly what he was imaging.

I recall another instance where a European had experimentally presented some African students with a picture, and asked them what they thought it represented. The picture was called *The Rescue* (the title was covered up) and showed in the foreground an exhausted mariner on a wrecked sailing-boat, while in the distance a small steamer could be seen approaching. The African students ventured to suggest it was a picture of fishing. This is wholly understandable.

Africans on Lake Victoria paddle about in canoes; they are sometimes drowned, but they do not spend days drifting on a wreck. Sailing-boats generally belong to the members (European) of the sailing-club. Small steamers are the normal transport for cargoes and passengers for longer journeys, and apart from such journeys the African goes to the lake to fish. They had translated the picture in terms of known imagery and concepts. This also indicates the many dangers attendant upon the European faith in pictures. It must be remembered that in this instance the Africans concerned were teachers in training and comparatively sophisticated. We can imagine how much more puzzling the picture might have been to a schoolchild from a bush school where his familiarity with the medium would have been infinitely less.

If imagery is the capital or food of imagination, a rich imagination signifies a rich store or reservoir of imagery to draw upon. Hence we must remember that an African child's sense experiences, and his reservoir of imagery and association (including of course emotional association) are very different in content from those of his European neighbour. This is clearly shown in the examples already quoted. It seemed to me that the first step in tackling the question of how to encourage imaginative work in African children, was to broaden the children's sensuous response to common objects by drawing their attention to them: that is, to develop awareness or consciousness, not (in the first instance) by the unfamiliar and second-hand medium of pictures, but by actual things and situations. (I found that tactile images seemed most in evidence.) You cannot, for example, explain to a child, in words, what the word 'prickly' means, but you can bring a pineapple into the class and hand it round the room and say, 'The sensation that you feel in your hands is what we call "prickly".'

It would seem not unreasonable to suggest that a lot of trouble could be saved if teachers of English would make an effort to learn the vernacular, and, instead of carting pineapples about, merely say, '"prickly" is what you call "a maggwa" in Luganda'. It is not as simple as that; Luganda is a difficult language, unrelated to any European tongue, and there are few teachers available who even dimly appreciate what difficulties Luganda presents to a European. (How often must Africans think this about us and our language!) But there is a far greater difficulty inherent in the language itself—namely the difference already stressed in associations and concepts. There are hardly any simple adjective stems in Luganda. (There is, for example, no word for 'square'. Naturally not. Until the arrival of foreigners, Africans in this part of the world lived in round huts, goods were carried on the head in round bundles on round pads, and vessels for food and drink were round.) The expression for 'prickly' in Luganda is 'of the prickle', and this concept does not, in fact, correspond to the European idea of 'prickly'. This is more clearly seen when a European tries to use the Luganda 'of the prickle' in situations where a European would say 'prickly'.

Add to that a most important point: African children have not consciously considered pineapples in terms of prickliness, nor egg-plants in terms of cool smoothness, nor tomatoes in terms of glowing colours. *That* approach is a strange one for them as they have been in the habit of thinking of all these things merely in terms of food. They have not thought of food in terms of aesthetic experience. It is easier to arouse a response to the quality of the juiciness in a pineapple than to its prickliness or the decorativeness of the tuft of frilly leaves at the top.

Here again, when teaching an English child the French for 'prickly', the teacher builds on the fact that he takes it for granted that an English child is aware of prickliness; and though he may associate it most strongly with, say brambles and blackberrying, it is easy for him to make the transfer and appreciate its connection with the rough scratchy skin and leaf-tufts of pineapples.

It may be argued that an African child is aware of the quality of prickliness of cactuses and prickly pears for instance, as he has good reasons for avoiding them because of this outstanding characteristic. It is precisely because such prickly plants fit into his pattern of sense responses as something to be feared or left alone that the pineapple does not evoke in him a prickle-image: in a pineapple the prickliness is quite harmless and therefore not worth noticing—the arresting characteristic is the juice and thirst-quenching quality.

So far the problem has been discussed only in connection with concrete objects. The reader can imagine how much more involved the situation becomes when the teacher tries to deal with abstractions such as 'friendship' or 'honour' (presupposing a completely different cultural background), or a simple adjective such as 'kind' (where the Luganda word also covers the European concepts 'generous, charming, attractive, gracious, indulgent, propitiatory', and many others). Add to this the whole range of vocabulary and concepts dealing with emotion, and the problem becomes indeed a formidable one.

In most tribal societies feelings are ritualized and emotions, in a sense, are 'prescribed'. If a wife loses a husband she must express grief in the expected way (beating her breast, wailing, rolling on the floor) and it becomes impossible to detect whether, behind the formalized ritualistic grief, there is or is not any real feeling (in the European sense). In the children's work one constantly gets sentences such as, 'My beloved mother died and I was sad for a whole week. I even did not eat any food'. And it is impossible to gauge the emotion or feeling according to any familiar European concepts. This is where one feels deeply one's own limitations in appreciating such unfamiliar manifestations and the exact nature of what gives rise to them.

On the other hand I found one of the younger boys sitting shivering by himself on a lump of concrete in the playground; when I asked him whether he was ill, he said his mother was dead. The statement is always stark and one meets only the prescribed and customary forms of expression.

Finally we decided to approach our problems as follows:

(1) Our first step must be to use every opportunity of extending our pupils' sense experiences, and of drawing their attention to these experiences. This would help to lead to the next stage.

(2) The reflection upon experience; the act of imagination (as opposed to 'imaging', that is, merely calling up images), is in itself a mental activity, a reflection on one's store of imagery and associations. This reflection could then find expression in different ways, three of the most easily recognizable being: (*a*) the modification of future behaviour in the light of this reflection on past experiences (foresight); (*b*) the application of this reflection to solve a problem, often in an apparently startling manner (insight); (*c*) the creating of something new or original out of this reservoir of imagery and association (creative activity). The reservoir alone is only half the answer; it is what the owner does with the contents that supplies the other half. On the other hand no-one can do anything with an empty tank.

(3) We must enable the child to become articulate, and to be able to express himself fearlessly on the subject of his sense perceptions and his reflections upon them.

(4) Lastly, we as teachers would need to develop in ourselves the imaginative insight able to recognize the rich variety of manifestations of different kinds of imagination unfamiliar to us.

To tackle these problems and the difficulties attendant upon them presented a formidable undertaking. Moreover there is always the voice of the devil. It was a sore temptation to satisfy oneself that, after all, one was doing a reasonable job in just teaching the children a sufficiency of what Sir Herbert Read has so aptly described as 'the prose of expediency' as opposed to 'the prose of Art'.[1] The former would serve for examinations and for limited daily use—why bother further?

It would have been all too easy to let oneself slide into one or other of the various groups of those who had already had dealings with African children and who claimed to 'know' about them. The two groups most frequently consist of:

(*a*) those who claim that African children have no imagination (though what exactly is meant by 'imagination' in this

[1] Herbert Read, 'English Prose' in *A Coat of Many Colours* (1945)

context it is difficult to ascertain) and that one should stick to the word-counts, and not launch into high falutin' nonsense;

(*b*) those who claim that African children are imaginative 'just like European children' (this is always intended as a compliment), and who produce in evidence some distressing imitations of what is believed to be 'European school-boys' imaginative writing'.

These two groups correspond perhaps to what Cohen has defined as 'The near-sighted positivists who call themselves realists (because they do not see the full reality) and the lazy dreamers who call themselves idealists (because they do not grapple with basic ideas)'.[1]

Another difficulty was caused by the desire to believe that African children possessed the same powers of creative imagination as European children. This made me doubly suspicious of deceiving myself into seeing expressions of creative imagination where none existed; or of projecting my own western imagination into what I read or saw; or, on the other hand, of missing the real signs on account of the unfamiliarity of the manifestations.

And behind all the technical difficulties already mentioned lay a profound philosophical difficulty, concerned with what Dr. Albert Schweitzer has defined as 'reverence for life'. The Christian concept of the sanctity of the individual is foreign to members of a tribal society, and even when that society begins to break down it probably remains one of the most difficult concepts for them to understand or accept. But it is this philosophical concept which lies at the root of that educational principle proclaimed in such statements as 'Every man is his own artist' (Herbert Read). The truth of this lies in the extent to which the individual follows his own perceptions, imagery and feelings, and, in creating something out of them, makes his unique contribution, however humbly, to the imaginative heritage of his race.

Perhaps it would be pertinent to conclude with the quotation

[1] Cohen, *Reason and Nature*, ch. 4 (Free Press, 1953).

from Emerson's *The Method of Nature* which heads Professor E. A. Wilson's chapter 'Man' in *The Miraculous Birth of Language*, a book which we have had good reason to read and re-read.

The termination of the world in a man appears to be the last victory of intelligence . . . . The great Man of old, who was clothed *in a leopard-skin to signify the beautiful variety of things*, and the firmament, his coat of stars—was but the representative of thee, O rich and various Man! thou palace of sight and sound, carrying in thy senses the morning and the night and the unfathomable galaxy; in thy brain the geometry of the City of God; in thy heart the bower of Love and the realms of right and wrong.

An individual man is a fruit which it cost all the foregoing ages to form and ripen. . . . Each individual soul is such, in virtue of its being power to translate the world into some particular language of its own.

Our problem then was to discover that particular language for African children—to each African child, his own individual language.

PART I

THE PROBLEM IN LANGUAGE TEACHING

I

DEVELOPING AN APPROACH TO THE PROBLEM

Language is the key to the heart of a people. If we lose the key we lose the people. If we treasure the key and keep it safe, it will unlock the door to untold riches, riches which cannot be guessed at from the other side of the door. This much I had learnt in over twenty years of language teaching, so that I approached the question of teaching English to African children with considerable trepidation, for I did not know one word of the vernacular.

When the children arrived in the school:

(*a*) They 'knew', that is had memorized 'parrot-fashion', something of almost everything, and 'understood', it seemed, almost nothing at all. Hence they were in a state of considerable confusion.

(*b*) They did not appear to expect to associate either 'meaning' or 'enjoyment' with language work. Hence many were listless and apathetic.

Owing to the nature of the situation in which we found ourselves, which included our own ignorance of Luganda, both my young colleague and I were debarred at the beginning from approaching the problem through the children's mother tongue. This was something that might be remedied later, but for the time being our immediate problem was to provide the children with at least some facility in the English language by making them fluent at a very simple level. There could be no expression without first achieving some sort of ease.

Somehow we had to replace the tense, sticky, un-English utterances, in so far as there were any at all, by something relaxed and enjoyable. At the same time it would be psychologically necessary to convey to our pupils that we were fully and consciously sympathetic to their mother tongue for which we must foster respect and awareness; and that in teaching them a foreign language totally different from an African language, we did at least realize some of the difficulties it would present to them. Later we might hope, by acquiring some knowledge of the vernacular, to get a better understanding of the specific difficulties which Baganda and local African children encountered in their learning of English. At all costs the problem must be approached open-mindedly and with the greatest flexibility. We recognized that in each child we were not approaching a *tabula rasa* but a mind full, however unconsciously, of linguistic concepts, attitudes and associations, many, if not most, of which would at least at this stage be unfamiliar to us. So unfamiliar indeed did they prove to be, that we found the expression of them, in extreme cases, aroused annoyance or antipathy in ourselves. Once we had recognized and analyzed this reaction it was one we could guard against, or at least treat with a degree of detachment. It is sobering to remember that, as Callan[1] has pointed out, the dictum 'I know what I like' attains universal truth when read to mean 'I like what I know'—that is, what is familiar and so reassuring and comfortable to me. The teacher is also human and can fall a prey to his emotions, antagonistic or otherwise, as easily as his pupils.

We envisaged that at the end of a period of about two years it might be possible, in the light of what we had learned from our pupils, to make a tentative plan for the approach to English teaching, this plan to be extended, altered and revised continually in the light of additional experience. We realized

[1] Norman Callan, *Poetry in Practice* (1938).

that we must keep clear of all educational and language-teaching 'fashions' and 'crazes', and steadfastly pursue the one basic principle of studying the needs peculiar to the particular group of children entrusted to us.

There was another practical issue to be considered. The children in a Secondary school would be faced with an examination within three years (later altered to two years) of their arriving at the school. This examination was a selective one, which would either enable them to continue their secondary education or would debar them for ever from enjoying such benefits. Whatever we decided was in the best interests of the pupils with regard to their education in the English language, we must see that this did not in any way penalize them from the examination point of view, as their futures depended on their performance. We were not unduly worried by this as, mercifully, what is sound educationally mostly reaps its reward in any examination worthy of the name. Any H.M.I. knows it is the feckless teacher's heaven-sent excuse to be able to point out mournfully what an excellent teacher he could be if only he were not hamstrung by examinations malevolently conceived to frustrate him.

We felt that we must at all costs associate the language work, (*a*) with real-life situations, not pictures; (*b*) with imaginative situations in which the pupils could participate. Our aim at all times was to link the new and as yet unknown to the known, and to extend their grasp of, and participation in, both the world of daily life and the world of imagination.

We were determined to give our pupils language teaching that was the best as we knew it. It was to be *education in and through language*, not merely chilly and soulless instruction in any particular European techniques. We hoped to achieve, through experience, a desirable balance and relationship between oral and written work. Owing partly to lack of money, and partly to other factors, few Primary schools had been able to give the children any adequate practice in written work, so that most children had no visual image for the sound of the word, nor any kinasthetic experience of it. In addition, for most of them it was the first time that they heard these sounds pronounced by a European, so they were naturally confused and puzzled.

If our aim was to give '*education* in the language' as opposed to '*instruction* in the language' then it was most important for us to remain highly critical, above all self-critical.

The greatest danger the teacher with integrity has to guard against is glibness, a comfortable acceptance of plausible dicta without proper investigation. This danger is greatly increased in a young country like Uganda, which inevitably provides a happy hunting-ground and battlefield for theories, prophecies and prejudices especially in the sphere of education. Mencken has pointed out that the greatest victim of prejudice is he who denies having any.[1] The most we could hope to do, therefore, was to remain aware of this inescapable factor and to approach our responsibilities with determination; to try and remain clear-sighted about the needs of our pupils and ready to cast aside any theory or axiom concerning language-teaching if it seemed seriously to interfere with the fulfilment of these needs. In working out our approach, therefore, we gave careful consideration to the following relevant points:

(1) Our pupils would be approaching their second language, not as a 'tabula rasa' as does the baby, for instance, in acquiring his mother tongue, but with a mind already full of language-habits and concepts. Moreover, any second experience, for psychological reasons, can never be the same as the first.

Cassirer has thrown light on these difficulties:

> In a later and more advanced state of our conscious life we can never repeat the process which led to our first entrance into the world of human speech. In the freshness, in the agility and elasticity of early childhood this process had a quite different meaning. Paradoxically enough *the real difficulty consists much less in the learning of the new language than in the forgetting of the former one.* [My italics.] We are no longer in the mental condition of the child who for the first time approaches a conception of the objective world. To the

[1] Mencken, *Selected Prejudices.*

adult or older child the objective world already has definite shape as a result of speech activity which has in a sense moulded all our other activities. Our perceptions, intuitions, and concepts have coalesced with the terms and speech forms of our mother tongue. Great efforts are required to realise the bond between words and things. And yet, when we set about to learn a new language, we have to make such efforts, and to separate the two elements.[1]

The significance and importance to children of 'first experiences' and their emotional associations, includes the profoundly important question of motivation. The baby learning to talk is dominated by the strongest of all human motives, the passionate desire to communicate and 'join in', and to get what he wants. This is a dynamic force, in the sense that psychologically speaking every situation is in fact unique. Even where there are similar elements in subsequent situations there cannot be a repetition in the exact and true sense of the word. No-one exemplifies this better than Helen Keller who has movingly and vividly described the situation of a child deprived of expression and shut out from 'joining in'.

Meanwhile the desire to express myself grew. The few signs I used became less and less adequate, and my failures to make myself understood were invariably followed by outbursts of passion. I felt as if invisible hands were holding me, and I made frantic efforts to free myself. I struggled—not that struggling helped matters, but the spirit of resistance was strong within me; I generally broke down in tears and physical exhaustion. If my mother happened to be near I crept into her arms too miserable even to remember the cause of the tempest. After a while the need of some means of communication became so urgent that these outbursts occurred daily, sometimes hourly.[2]

(2) We wished to keep a firm grip on the two main strands of language-development, (*a*) spoken expression; (*b*) written expression. In the history of the race as well as in the history of the individual the written word evolved after speech, and this helps us to establish their respective spheres of operation.

[1] Cassirer, 'Language,' in *Essay on Man*, p. 33. (New York, 1944).

[2] Helen Keller, *The Story of My Life*, p. 23 (1947).

The immediate urgency of a language is communication of daily needs. Oral language is primarily 'functional language', and as such is to be found among all non-literate peoples. But as soon as the need arises for the expression of thoughts of a deeper and more complex nature, a different and more permanent form of expression is sought.

It is interesting to compare the following quotations:

Writing and printing are only speech reduced to black signs.[1]

And now we come to the final step in the making of language. By the conventionalization of sound in oral speech, which is the actual language, man accomplished two things ....

But this conventionalization of sound in oral speech did not completely solve the problem set to conscious reason, of raising above the transient world of nature a permanent and actual world of mind.... There was no independent objective permanence at all in oral language. The only permanence was in the memory of the living individual that could produce the language again when it was required. Without the presence of the living human agent the thing had completely vanished.

But the characteristics of the world of mind, as already noted, is that it combines permanency with motion.

To obtain the required permanence the time symbols of oral speech had to be converted in some way or other into space symbols, since space has that fixity which time lacks. Hence all nations that made any considerable advance in the elaboration of their mental world were led by instinct and necessity to search for some kind of space symbols, written speech as we now call it, that would crystallize and hold the vanishing streams of oral speech.

The conversion of the sound-symbols of time into corresponding form-symbols of space, which gave to language an accumulating permanence without destroying or altering its life and movement, was the most momentous and fruitful single achievement of the human intellect, since it was the condition of all cumulative progress that man has since made in the world of free mind, which is his peculiar sphere.[2] [My italics.]

Written expression is the result of reflection on experience and is likely to be richer in thought and imagination than

[1] F. B. French, C.B.E., *The Teaching of English Abroad*, Pt. 1, p. 6. (1948).

[2] R. A. Wilson, *The Miraculous Birth of Languages*, p. 174 ff. (London Guild Book No. 213).

speech. The three great literary art-forms of a people's written literature, Prose, Drama and Poetry, clearly reflect this, and cannot, of course, be regarded merely as 'Speech written down'. We wished, therefore, to proceed to develop the spoken and written word as complementary aspects of human expression, both forms having their proper function. We planned a two-fold approach to our English teaching, through which we hoped that the 'prose of expediency' would be supplemented by 'the prose of art', the latter being, as we conceived it, the prose of reflection and imagination.

(3) It cannot be reiterated too often that in teaching a foreign or second language, as in all other spheres of teaching, the teacher must be clear in his own mind as to the end or aim of his teaching so that he can use the appropriate means to achieve these ends. Different groups of people learn languages with different ends in view.

I was once asked to conduct a course in the German language for air pilots and others who might shortly find themselves literally precipitated into a different country. Clearly in such a situation it would be unrealistic, and unfair to the learners, to do anything other than to analyse the particular real-life situations in which they might soon find themselves; to equip them with the vocabulary and structures suited to such situations; and to make all this compatible with the learning time at one's disposal. This is necessarily a quantitative and utilitarian approach and one which is wholly justifiable in certain circumstances; for instance in the case of selected groups of adults who require to learn a foreign language for specific and limited purposes. However, this approach must be applied with sensitivity and discretion when the aim is *education* in and through the language, and not mere *instruction* of a limited kind. In this case a proper balance and proportion between the quantitative and qualitative approach must be established.

The principle of word-frequency is the hall-mark of the quantitative approach, and while its limitations are now more generally recognized, this was far from being the case at the time it was introduced in Uganda. (The Thorndike word-count was the one most generally advocated.) Here too we concluded that the most useful word-counts were those one made and selected oneself to fit the needs of one's own pupils, altering them as further experience threw further light on those needs.

There are, however, other qualitative aspects of 'words', which have a far greater influence on the ease with which the learner remembers them; their emotional or symbolic associations are an example (the Jungian word-association tests depend on this factor). There is also the 'sound' aspect of words, their rhythm and onomatapœia. I had always found in teaching French and German that these aspects had a far greater significance for the children than the mere frequency aspect of words. The less usual word of high emotive or rhythmic power would 'stick' more readily than the word of high frequency. This same principle is embodied also in the more recent approach to reading material in infant schools, where sentences such as 'Elizabeth has a doll called Jemima' now feature in place of 'The cat sat on the mat'. This is not to say that in oral work a word which is constantly required is not also readily remembered through use, but that other aspects of words are as important, if not more important, especially when applied to the prose of reflection.

We therefore planned to make a study of the special appeal that such words might have for African children, and to include them in our graded vocabulary. We hoped in this way to combine the vocabulary of everyday activities with the vocabulary of literature.

(4) Lastly we wished to observe and analyse carefully what kind of activity connected with language learning might prove to be of value to African children. In the light of past European experience we were fully aware that the principle of activity for acitivity's sake (that is, the abuse of the activity principle), can prove as deadening as the passivity the principle is intended to counteract. In the educational field the cry 'God save me from

my disciples', may justifiably be uttered with more than usual poignancy, and John Dewey's case has been put by Aldous Huxley:

> Under the influence of John Dewey [the exponents of Progressive Education] have stressed the importance of non-verbal activity as a means of learning. The important point, in our present context, is that the doing through which the children are supposed to learn, is left unanalysed by the progressive educators who advocate it. So far as they are concerned, doing is doing; there is nothing to choose between one kind of doing and another. John Dewey himself knew better but his following have chosen to plunge headlong and with unquestioning enthusiasm into their mud-pies.[1]

We were determined to guard against *indiscriminate* 'doing'. Though the 'mud-pies' refer of course to the indiscriminate messing of the 'project method' when uncritically applied, doing for doing's sake has spread to all spheres of teaching including language-teaching. Naturally any serious teacher accepts the axiom that his pupils should be actively involved in the learning-teaching situation, but the misapplication of the principle can lead to some gruesome abuses. For instance, in the English course which was almost universally used in Uganda and which claimed to have been especially written for Africa, the following type of activity is advocated:

Sit on the table Stand on the desk	Book 1. Lesson 9. Pupil's book.
Draw six bad balls	Book 1. Lesson 17. Pupil's book.
Draw two eggs, a fat gourd, seven balls	Book 1. Lesson 20. Pupil's book.
Stand on the chair Kick the desk Hit that boy (or girl) Put the pencil in the ink Show me the picture of an ass	Book 1. Lesson 24. Pupil's book.
Kick something long	Book 1. Lesson 45. Pupil's book.

In 1957 this text-book formed the English syllabus for Uganda. This course was in six books and intended to cover six

[1] Aldous Huxley, *Adonis and the Alphabet* (1956).

years of learning. It proved to be one of the most serious obstacles we had to contend with in trying to achieve our aims.

Text-books in general are easy Aunt Sallies but the few examples quoted may perhaps indicate something of the nature of the problem presented.

Children are tough and survive a great deal, but African children, so newly introduced to formal education, are more vulnerable than most. One does not wish to over-estimate the influence of a text-book; but it would be a mistake also to under-estimate the cumulative effect of several years of the type of 'learning' illustrated above, especially as this course was often the sole source of study. Europeans are sometimes inclined to reproach Africans for their inability to think for themselves and for lacking initiative; we might perhaps ask ourselves whether we, the educators, are entirely free from responsibility in the matter.

As may be imagined, our own problem of how to teach African children their second language, in a way which encouraged their imaginative faculties and the spontaneous expression of them, was considerably aggravated by their previous experience in learning English. There was, among a host of other 'taught' inaccuracies and misconceptions, the really serious difficulty caused by the inculcation (in 54 lessons) of the Present Continuous tense, that is, the least and one of the most idiomatically used tenses in the English language. This also grew out of the 'activities' illustrated above. If one is constantly asking the question, 'What are you doing?' in an artificially created situation (as opposed to a real-life situation) this involves answering in replies equally divorced from real-life situations, for example, 'I was standing up', 'I am sitting down'. In real life we do not make such comments, nor do people with normal vision ask the question with a view to obtaining such an answer.

In 1957 I was teaching in a Primary school where the habit of using the wrong tense was already ingrained in Class V. In the classroom where I taught, the wooden shutters, which had broken fasteners, used to bang to, making the room very dark and sometimes upsetting the girls. On one such occasion, realizing that a girl at the back of the room was distracted, and unable in the general murkiness to see what the trouble was, I asked the girl, in this genuine real-life context, 'Naomi, what are you doing?' This immediately triggered off the conditioned reflex, 'I am sitting down'. When I retorted irritably, 'Don't be silly, I can see that. I want to know what you are *doing*', a complete impasse of non-communication was established and I had to resort to asking the question in Luganda whereupon I immediately received an intelligent answer. She said in Luganda, 'I have lost my pen'.

The implications of this are important, for it is clear that the pupil associated *sense* and *meaning* with the mother tongue, whereas only *meaningless drill* was associated with English. This is the foreseeable result of 'teaching-by-the-book', where the book is earnestly pursuing the 'learning-by-doing' and picture-describing method, without any regard for meaning in real-life situations. Creating totally artificial situations in the classroom which have no meaningful parallel situations in everyday life lays the most undesirable of all foundations, namely one which has to be dug up and relaid.

Summing up our position *vis-à-vis* the four beliefs just examined, we entered into the question of teaching English to African children:

(1) aware that this second language could not be acquired in the same way as the child's mother tongue, and that we should have to give careful consideration to the balance between conscious and unconscious learning;

(2) aware that we must achieve a desirable balance between oral 'functional' speech and writing (the prose of expediency), and more complex written, imaginative expression (the prose of reflection);

(3) aware that we must keep in mind the balance between the quantitative and qualitative approach to vocabulary and structures ('patterns');

(4) aware of the dangers of an unanalysed 'activity' approach with (in our special context) particular reference to describing pictures, whether wall-pictures or illustrations in text-books. (It must be remembered that no-one would describe a picture to another person, except, perhaps, to someone who is blind, or absent—for example a commentator at a football match on the radio. A mother with a young child on her knee might do the same with a picture-book but these are special situations which, we felt, should not take priority when teaching African children English.)

We then made our plans based on previous experience of teaching English, French and German to European children, but adapted, as far as our knowledge at that time would permit, to meet the needs of our African pupils. We were ready to re-adapt or alter them radically, as required.

I had never at any time when teaching languages used a set 'Course'. I had been trained not to do so by a linguist and practising teacher of definite views to whom 'Courses' were anathema. This was because naturally no course is designed for a specific group of pupils. Its sales value lies in its relative applicability to the maximum possible number of varying groups of pupils, and in this case the pupils are entirely at the mercy of the intelligence and sympathy of the teacher in adapting the course to their particular needs. No 'Course' which is rigidly adhered to and enforced can possibly be fulfilling specific needs. Moreover it had been impressed on me during my training in linguistic method that what was left out when teaching a language was every bit as important as what was put in. Courses only too frequently sin in both directions, but most particularly in including things the experienced teacher prefers to keep secret until his pupils have reached the linguistic maturity which justifies the corresponding linguistic revelation. In any form of teaching, ripeness is all. There is probably more wastefulness in teaching through ignoring this vital principle than through ignoring any other similar one. I had been told that I could have as many 'Courses' as I liked on my bookshelf at home, and I could select from them anything that appeared useful and pertinent, but that the children must build up their own 'Course' from a carefully graded syllabus compiled by the teacher through his reading and experience, in a specially designed 'Language-book'. What went into the pupil's own language-book was carefully selected material related to the oral and written work, which was entered by the pupils themselves, the aim being that nothing went into this book which was not understood and practised by the pupils; understanding being principle number one.

I had found this method very rewarding educationally and, applied to French and German, gratifying in its examination results, a matter not to be despised at a time when teachers who did not produce desirable examination results lost their jobs. At a later stage, teaching English in England, I used this approach again.

It therefore seemed sensible to base our teaching of English to African children on the same method; it was the only one known to me which combined absolute attention to the special needs of a specific group of pupils, with the flexibility essential in a situation where so much was unknown to us and where clearly the 'Course' or 'Syllabus' would have to be continually modified to meet these needs. If we failed in this basic essential then all our efforts would be wasted.

It was also the only method, of which I had experience, which enabled the teacher to treat all reading and writing as 'literature', that is, creatively and imaginatively.

Our approach then was a two-fold one:

(1) Language through real-life situations (situational English).

(2) Language through literature (the prose of reflection and imagination).

Our scheme eventually took shape under six headings:

(1) *Language-work*, that is 'grammar'—in pupils' own language book.

(2) *Oral work:*

(i) Real-life situations' method (situational English), for example—At the grocer's
In the Post Office
Looking for a pen, etc.
How to write letters.

(ii) Comprehension:
Questions and answers on literature that had been read, also on specially selected comprehension passages.

(iii) Oral composition:
Preparation for certain kinds of written composition.

(iv) Reproduction:
Retelling a story or parts of a story in connection with the literature that had been read.

(v) Reading:
Pupils reading aloud in turn what had already been read aloud by the teacher. (We had about two reading tests a term.)

(vi) Poetry:
Choral speaking and acting.

(vii) Acting (in the vernacular and English);
(*a*) Acting of stories and using puppets
(*b*) Puppet and drama club.

(3) *Written work*:

(i) Written exercises to practise specific language points that had been put in the language-book.

(ii) Composition:
(*a*) Original and imaginative writing (with oral preparation).
(*b*) Written reproduction of story or part of story read (first prepared orally).
(*c*) Written dialogues on real-life (first prepared orally).

(iii) Dictation (usually made up by the teacher to contain points required).

(iv) Written questions in connection with literature that had been read.

(4) *Text books.*

(5) *Vocabulary.*

(6) *Remedial teaching* (elimination of technical and conceptual errors).

The key to the written work, however, lay in the carefully graded composition work which we regarded as the touchstone of all our efforts. We used the selected graded vocabulary and structures or 'patterns' we had evolved for the pupils, which were drawn from two sources; (i) real-life situations; and (ii) reading in prose, poetry, and drama.

Of the headings above, only those most nearly relevant to the problem of original imaginative work with African children will be dealt with in this book. In a sense, all have a bearing on the problem, but if all were considered this would involve writing a book on language-teaching alone.

When my colleague and I arrived at the school, we were startled to find that, apart from the officially prescribed 'English Course', the reading texts available were strange in their vocabulary, ranging from Edwardian slang to full-scale bogus 'period-language'. They included, for instance, some emasculated Conan Doyle with lots of the 'My dear Watson' humour. They were, as we saw it, completely and absolutely removed from the children's actual experience, and from any possibility of their imaginative participation. They were not, in fact, *meaningful.*

We jettisoned all this printed matter, though not without apprehension as these texts were universally accepted, used and recommended.

We then combed the local book-shops. We had attempted to discover what kind of 'Oral Literature' in the form of story-telling and so on was known to exist among the Baganda and other local tribes. We examined books containing Bantu proverbs and songs, of which there were translations available. Spontaneous ceremonial chants, recorded by anthropologists, were, as might be imagined, of a nature which precluded their use in schools. However, we were not looking at these things from the point of view of using them in school, for their very familiarity might make them stale. We were endeavouring to find a point from which we could extend the children's imaginative experience, and this meant 'buttoning-on' our literature to what was there already, and what could be expected to rouse their interest.

Having considered all the available information, and it was thread-bare enough, we decided to embark, in the first instance, on such fairy-tales or folk-tales or legends as could be collected, making sure that they were written simply, but not inanely. The art of writing simply without using a vocabulary and style which are a barely hidden insult to the reader, however much of a beginner he may be, is an art to which far too little attention has been paid.

The first question always asked about a story (we had reached questions by this time) was, 'Madam, is it true?' In the case of fairy-tales one explained that there were different sorts of truth and that fairy-tales and legends embodied a kind of truth or wisdom resulting from man's experience and concerning certain types of behaviour and their consequences. For example, the youngest son, laughed at by his more handsome and powerful brothers, through his humanity and kindness to the little old man in the forest, is rewarded by such things as success in human relationships, happy marriage, friendship and popularity. These explanations were always listened to with great attention and accepted with apparent satisfaction, and the expression, often directly out of the story, 'because he had a good heart', or 'because he had a warm heart', was always effortlessly assimilated and used. The language, particularly of Grimm's fairy-tales, was also soaked up. Sometimes, quite surprisingly, whole paragraphs were memorized. There were, as far as we could judge, two main reasons for this. (*a*) The content somehow made an emotional impression; for example the two paragraphs in 'Hansel and Gretel', first where the wife nags the husband about getting rid of the children, and second, where the children are abandoned in the forest, seemed to have an exceptional effect on the children. (*b*) The rhythm of the sentences and evocativeness of the words and idioms were the cause of the appeal. In the first instance it is as well to remember that many African children are sent to relations or respected friends, away from home and their parents, either to attend school or for some other reason. They usually have to work for their keep. In the pupil's original writing, more especially and revealingly in what they wrote under the title of 'A chapter out of my autobiography', the fear of 'unkind masters' was the one most frequently expressed. They also often described the situation where their 'master' or 'uncle' or his wife showed discrimination between his own children and those who were, so to speak, billetted on him. This discrimination was most bitterly resented when expressed in terms of meanness with regard to food. The theme of the wicked step-mother, therefore, was one which touched them personally.

We were often in the dark concerning the second point, the extraordinary charm that certain kinds of language had for them. Often we could not understand the peculiar attraction of these words and phrases, because they did not (in our experience) exercise this influence on European children. Conversely, of course, passages and expressions which affected European children often made no impression whatever on our African pupils. Many of our pupils came from mission schools and were most familiar with the language of the Bible, with its simple directness and rhythm, and parabolic teaching. We thought that similar qualities, found in the fairy-tales, may have made them feel at home. Certainly the reading had a remarkable and most happy effect on their own writing. The following very representative example is produced without alteration. It was written during an examination (and is therefore completely unaided) at the end of the first year's work, that is, at the end of Junior Secondary 1.

Once upon a time, there lived a poor woodcutter near a large forest. He had a wife and two children. The mother was not the real mother of the children. Their mother died when they were still very small.

Once there came a famine in the land. The poor woodcutter had not enough food for his wife, and himself, and his children. One day when he lay in the bed feeling very troubled, he said to his wife, 'What will become of us how can we feed our children when we have almost nothing for ourselves?'

The woman answered, 'I will tell you what to do.' She said 'We will take our children deeper into the forest. There we shall make fire for them, and they will be unable to come back.'

But the poor woodcutter said 'No I can't be cruel to take my children into the forest and leave them there, the wild animals will soon come and eat them.' But the woman said 'Oh you fool why have you refused to do such things? Then make some coffins for us.' After many things which the woman talked the poor woodcutter agreed to her plan.

The significant aspect of this is the standard of fluency and the obvious impression left by the picturesqueness of the imagery, that is the bit about preparing the coffins, which had clearly caught the writer's imagination, although very different from the local custom of burial.

We were for some time puzzled as to what literature to use in the second year after the fairy-tales and legends. In England it would have been the stage for adventure stories. (N.B. the 'stage', and not 'age'. The ages of African children cannot be thought of as parallel to those of European children, and it is always safer to talk in terms of development.) I also wanted to link this up with what I optimistically hoped might be taught at the same time in history, namely the explorations. But history was suffering from the same unimaginative approach as English, and there is a limit to what one can tackle at one time. In the event, all we could do was to consider the problem from the angle of English. Here we immediately came up against the question of what 'adventures' would have significance and interest for African children who lived themselves in a state of perpetual adventure, if that definition included danger, physical hardship, sudden illness, accidents and death. To European boys a wild pig hunt might be a thrill, to many rural African children it was a reality and meant, if they were lucky, meat for supper. When being hit on the head for your bicycle or having your house broken into with violence is not merely a reality but a constant threat, the romantic aspect of the adventure is apt to fade. Adventures on the sea were meaningless, and disguises beyond our pupils' grasp. Then we hit on *King Solomon's Mines.* This immediately became and remained a great favourite, largely on account of 'Gagool' (there was always some wretched boy nicknamed after her!) though all 'humorous' bits had to be skipped. I tried on several occasions to explain why English children thought them funny, but the blankness which met my attempts discouraged me so much that I gave it up.

Stories about animals, that happy source of reading for English children from every kind of social background, were useless here. That is, stories about animals as pets and friends of man, as opposed to animals personified in legends. Most Africans have no conception of the European love of animals, whether of the sentimental or genuine variety.

Finally I mercifully remembered the remarkable success of *Emil and the Detectives* in French and German, and so examined the English version. I was delighted to find it suitable in every age-group. 'That is a wonderful story', said one boy, in Senior 3, speaking from his heart. 'Please tell me, has that writer written any other stories, because I should like to read them?' I was continually being asked for the loan of the book after it had been read. The background, the situation, the train journey, the passengers, the money stolen on the train, everything 'clicked'. The sentence, 'The money was gone,' was received with deep groans and the expression 'tall stories' for the brand of taradiddle told by the thief to the little boy was greeted with delight and never forgotten. (Naturally no 'word-count' would contain such an idiom.) The town-boy's remark to Emil on finding he had just arrived in the city from the village, 'Is that why you're wearing such silly clothes?', brought the house down, and it was some time before order could be restored. These points all produced the same reactions when I read the book with a group of Primary school teachers; this might well serve as a pointer to teacher-trainers as to the kind of literature African teachers can be expected to teach with the understanding and sympathy needed in order to arouse a similar response in their pupils. A teacher who has no sympathy with his subject-matter is merely wasting his own and his pupils' time.

We then had to think of what might follow the first two stages. One had only to ponder the fantastic difficulties, physical and otherwise, to which many African children are subjected and which they have to struggle to overcome, to realize that autobiography and biographies dealing with similar hardships and struggles were likely to have an immediate appeal. They did.

African school-children sometimes cycle as many as twenty-six or more miles to school, soaked through in wet weather. They often have no light in their huts to study by on their return in the evening, even supposing they had the energy to do so. They are also usually obliged to do a fair number of household chores. Moreover they live in a disintegrating society, their fixed pattern of behaviour now shaken by a multiplicity of possible choices of untried patterns. They are therefore understandably and irresistibly drawn to the real-life story which embodies the fulfilment of their own dreams, the success and recognition attendant upon the individual's overcoming all the difficulties.

In the case of the autobiographies and biographies, we chose simplified versions of the lives of Marie Curie, Booker Washington and Helen Keller. All were successful in varying degrees, but Marie Curie almost became part of the lives of our pupils.

Our local African children were profoundly attracted to all things medical and scientific. In the first instance this was because these new professions offer great wealth and prestige, but secondly because the children identified themselves with the suffering. In *Marie Curie* almost every kind of suffering appears, most comprehensible being persecution, exile and the occupation of one's country by cruel and foreign conquerors.

The chapter describing the visit of the Russian Inspector, when the Polish books had to be secreted at the risk of death to teachers and pupils, caused horrified head-shaking. Our explanation that dictators and conquerors always attack schools and universities—where in a non-dictatorship the greatest measure of freedom is to be found—and also attempt to drive out the mother tongue of the conquered as this is their life-blood, was always received with appreciative understanding and sympathy. When it was pointed out that if a people occupying a country encouraged the acquisition of a second language, this was very different from forbidding all use of the mother tongue, amused appreciation would gradually spread over the pupils' faces. I am not likely to forget the reactions of the pupils to Marie Curie's poverty and freezing cold attic while studying in Paris; nor the intensely moving experience of looking up after reading the passage describing the death of Pierre Curie, to see the shocked and distressed faces and dark eyes brimming with tears. Africans seem to cry easily, but it was a genuine feeling nevertheless, evoked by something real. I could not help thinking of what Marie Curie herself would have felt had she been able to see the groping imaginative sympathy on those faces. When at the end of the book Marie Curie herself came to die it was even worse, and at all subsequent readings I had to steel myself for what was coming.

The girls loved the book for its portrayal of female emancipation and there was discussion on a subject near to their hearts—women's education. Surprise and relief were haltingly expressed when they realized that this kind of emancipation was by no means of very ancient origin in western countries.

The descriptions of home-life with the old widower, Sklodovski, were favourite passages and gave rise to many a tale of different customs in different countries. These were much welcomed by us as teachers; far too many Africans (and Europeans also) use the word 'European' as a synonym for 'English'. Our pupils were astonished when the error was pointed out and were eager to hear about other kinds of Europeans. All discussions concerning varying approaches to the all-important matter of food and drink were welcomed; the samovar was a happy starting-point and led to my describing, with drawings on the board, the various ways of making tea and coffee, and the kinds of food eaten with them in different parts of Europe. The French *baguette* or *couronne* never failed to strain their credulity to the utmost and I rather think at least half the class privately thought me a liar.

As Madame Curie's daughter, Madame Joliot-Curie, was working in Paris, I went to the Sorbonne when on leave and though unable to attend a lecture given by her, I saw her signature on the notice-board. On my return, I described this to the class and suggested they might like to write and tell Madame Joliot-Curie how much they had enjoyed her sister's book about their mother. Before this could be put into practice the news of Madame Joliot-Curie's death appeared in the paper. The announcement included the information that she had died, like her mother, for science, suffering from the same disease caused by her ceaseless research work on radium. This news made a very considerable impression on the children and brings home to the teacher how important it is for some of the literature studied in school to be closely associated with contemporary life and events, to help break down the (to us) almost inconceivable isolation of Africans.

At this point I feel I ought to make clear the enormous importance to the children of the book being read aloud by the teacher, both for enjoyment and extension of knowledge and understanding. We looked on these literature lessons as some of the most educative and, as they later proved to be, rewarding periods on the time-table. There was a comfortable atmosphere in the room as children settled themselves in their seats. The once mask-like faces that had defeated us in the early stages were now relaxed. The children reacted to the story with spontaneous noises (such as sighs, grunts and cluckings), and involuntary gestures. There was, in fact, varying in degree with each individual, imaginative participation.

It will be understood from all this that if children were left to read the story on their own, a practice much advocated by some educators and teachers, then from our point of view of trying to educate in and through language and literature, the whole point would be missed. One approach, which I feel to be singularly ill-considered with regard to young Africans, is that which advocates 'read extensively, get the general drift and never mind about the details'. Once, when I questioned an English teacher and Headmaster who was encouraging this approach in a secondary school, he said, 'But I want to get them into the *habit* of reading'. There is probably no habit more unfortunate for an African and the future of his country, than for him to get into the habit of thinking he has understood and grasped the meaning of something read, when the true meaning has eluded him. Such a habit is likely to have widespread and disturbing repercussions, and if we, as Europeans, are going to encourage it, we must ask ourselves if we are also prepared to answer for the results. As teachers, we were in no way attracted to the quantitative approach to reading, especially since, in the case of African children, it was more than doubtful if they would get anything whatsoever out of such 'reading on their own'. The reader who attempts to get the general drift of something too foreign for him, finds that when enough uncomprehended detail has piled up he has also lost sight of the general drift. However, later on, the experiment was tried and some of the children wrote what they thought about it. The following extracts are illuminating. (They are completely unaltered.)

(1) *By a boy in his fourth year of secondary schooling*

My opinion about the teaching of English literature of African pupils, is that we learn more when we read literature books with our teachers, because the teachers can give us satisfactory explanations, and *deep meanings of difficult words and complicated sentences* which we cannot understand by ourselves. Some books of School Certificate level are found so difficult that it takes a long time to understand the meaning and very often we get very crude explanations. *When we look up words that we don't know the meaning of in dictionaries, and we are very often led astray, because in many languages words give different ideas* and they are used to give different senses and meanings, which one cannot understand by himself if one wants to learn a foreign language, and indeed *dictionaries only help us to learn spelling of words* and perhaps give us meanings of words we are not very sure of, *but cannot teach us English if weve no teacher's help.* They can't give you deep meanings of for example metaphors and ideas used in the books, and looking up these words does not allow you to follow the book and it delays us very much as we have short time for the job. . . . There are some ideas, and simple library books. I do not mean that all of these should be read with teachers but these can be read and understood by a pupil so long as he can understand them because they can't spoil his English since they are simple and easy to understand and so the pupils should read these for themselves in their spare time.

I expect a pupil who is taught in such a way to be very good at English and I hope many support my idea. [My italics.]

It can be seen that the child himself distinguishes quite clearly in his own mind, however haltingly he expresses it, the type of book which is in itself an education and requires the assistance of the teacher, and very simple books on which to exercise his silent reading. As he points out, the latter 'can't spoil his English since they are simple and easy to understand'. The only books that help a pupil's silent reading are in fact those which are several stages behind his actual comprehension, and where both vocabulary and structures belong to what he has already fully mastered.

In addition to the spare time reading of simple reading-books, we encouraged the children to re-read the books studied with the teacher. Judging by subsequent questions, this proved both valuable and popular. One of the many rewards of teaching African children is to see the pleasure they experience in becoming aware of their increasing grasp of a book. They often made such comments as 'It is much easier now', or 'I begin to understand'. The comments were frequently accompanied by a satisfied stretch and friendly grin, expressing relief and confidence.

(2) *By a boy in his fourth year of secondary schooling*

It is better to read a Literature text with a teacher than to read it alone.

All best writers of books write with the intention of conveying some idea to the reader. Some of course differ from others in that the way in which they want to show their ideas to the reader is quite difficult.

It is wrongly thought that a young pupil by reading a class set-book, understands it well and gets through it without omitting important points. School children seem to know very little of the world and if a teacher goes on giving them books which they can read without difficulty, then all the time is wasted in giving them work they knew already.

One must always think that there are different people in a class. Some of course can pick up things quite easily and others can take a long time without understanding even the easiest points. If a teacher sits idle and does not come to the aid of the latter then the class will miss out the points and pleasures which the book was intended to give and all this will mean hatrage of the subject.

In some books all the amusements and the fun of it are centred around one fact, and if such a book as "The White Company" which is full of chivalry were given to read by an African boy without any assistance of a teacher it would be difficult to interest him, because all stories and legends from his ancestors have believed in the fact that women should obey men and honour them, and above all such a book was written with the intention of conveying the Middle Ages customs and policies, which would be difficult to understand to an African boy of the present Age.

A foreigner who is learning English finds a lot of difficulty in the pronouncing some words correctly, e.g. experience, language. It must not be forgotten that one learning a new language is always eager to use the new words he has learnt. Such words as "lingo, fondle, cogitate" are not easy to use, but on the other hand if he was told the correct way of using the word he would not misuse it. Also it seems to me as though a teacher is not interested in his work by giving books after books to the children. If you compare the answers of both students [He meant those who have done their reading with the teacher and those who haven't.] there is an enormous difference.

(3) *The following is from a boy in his third year of secondary schooling*

To read a book by oneself or to read it through with a teacher.

I positively prefer to read through a book with a teacher, the latter being the best appreciated even by my fellow pupils. I personally prefer it because one has all the chances of asking for the meanings of new words of phrases.

When I asked my class mates as to which of the two they preferred most, I found that all of them prefer to read with a teacher, and a few of the reasons they gave are as follows:—

[a][1] One of them said 'When I read a book by myself I meet the word which I cannot pronounce, whereas if there was a teacher reading, and me following in my book, I would learn the pronounciation of the word.'

[b] The other said, 'We are not likely to understand the meanings of all the English words we read in a book, and in my case when I meet such things I am forced to stop until I get someone to explain the meanings to me. A dictionary is useful when you have a new word, but where do you look for a phrase new to you?'

Another said, 'I may understand the meanings of some phrases, but when it comes to where they are used in different ways and different sentences I get mixed up completely.'

[c] And another said that when he reads a book by himself he must have a dictionary near him, and that, he says, confuses him a lot when he has to refer to it every minute.

After all these consultations, which showed at last that the difficulties stated could be solved by having a teacher reading with the pupils, I conclude that it is better to read a book with a teacher.

I have personally experienced both ways, and I have found how fruitless that one of reading by oneself is that I very much like, like most of the pupils do, the other way of reading a book with a teacher.

[a] This point about the pronunciation was also made by the writers of the other two extracts. It was not one which would have occurred to us, though in retrospect we did realize the

[1] Letters in square brackets refer to the comments on pp. 40-41.

children often asked us to repeat certain words and phrases which were then practised.

[b] It is as well to remember here that the advocators of extensive silent reading invariably reply to this argument of the child's, 'We don't expect you to understand every word, it doesn't matter'. They miss the vital point, which the child realizes full well, that if you do not get the correct meaning or significance of key words or phrases, the story very soon does not make sense. Ironically enough, the other argument brought forward in favour of this sort of reading is that it should be for leisure and enjoyment.

[c] Many of us will remember this type of misery when trying to read French books with only a dictionary for help. Constant reference to a dictionary cancels out enjoyment.

These essays not only show a good deal of shrewd observation but also how much the children appreciated the informality of the literature class discussions. They incidentally also show how much the children's thinking had benefited from these lessons.

There is one argument which is complacently put forward by those who hold that teaching language through literature is a piece of non-realistic nonsense, or at the least unpractical. It is the argument that this kind of teaching can only be done by a European anyway and that in view of the imminence of Africanization,[1] only those ways of teaching which can be carried on unaided, by an African teacher, should be handed on to African teachers in training. The European protagonists of this argument (and I am afraid I have met many) would consider the studying of the book *Marie Curie* a case in point. They would argue that only a European knows about samovars and the shapes of French bread and so, of course, he can get something out of the study of the book which an African teacher could not. This is, of course, quite true, but it is only one aspect of the question. Paradoxically enough, these arguers also as easily assert that samovars, etc., are of no significance anyway so the child might just as well read the book on his own.

[1] Since the time of writing Uganda has celebrated her independence.

There are chiefly two counter-arguments one would like to put forward. The first is that while there are still Europeans teaching in the schools it would seem pointless to prevent them from teaching what they (allegedly) alone can teach. Such an argument is not the kind of argument which cuts much ice in other spheres (that is non-educational spheres). A doctor would not argue that because he only has enough of a certain drug to save one patient he must therefore abstain from using it on the one, since this would be unfair to those he cannot save.

Secondly, what an African teacher can be expected to teach depends both on his natural ability and on his training. The whole question of what books can be studied with African teachers of English in training so that they can afterwards study these with their pupils, is one which requires thoughtful consideration and investigation (that is not Gallup Polls and questionnaires). 'Just as eating contrary to the inclination is injurious to the health, so study without desire spoils the memory, and it retains nothing that it takes in', says Leonardo De Vinci, writing five centuries ago.[1] If teachers in training study books which are either beyond their imaginative participation or are inane and superficial, they will find these books meaningless. This will result either in total loss, or else in meaningless learning by rote. This latter will in turn reappear in the classroom as learning by rote, and thus a particularly vicious circle will be perpetuated.

We felt it was not unreasonable to believe that what deeply impressed the children would also be equally teachable to students in training and in that case the whole business of 'handing on' both new factual knowledge and sympathetic interpretation would be accomplished. There is always a certain margin of loss (but sometimes also of gain) in all forms of handing on.

Returning now to the texts, in the fourth year we introduced *Cry, the Beloved Country*, but I was not at all sure that this was satisfactory. What gradually became more and more clear was

[1] Leonardo Da Vinci, *Notebooks* (1938).

that African children do not want stories about Africa. They know it all too well. We detected a psychological resistance (unconscious I am sure), which we put down to their feeling that patronizing if well-intentioned Europeans imagined this was just the right literature for Africans. I made up my mind to find something different, and if my work had continued I should not have repeated *Cry, the Beloved Country*, except experimentally.

After that we started on the School Certificate texts, as nothing upset our African school-children more than to be flustered by lack of time. They must be allowed to absorb literature in comfort and leisure, but without dragging. The Cambridge School Certificate examination offered an alternative syllabus for Literature which we welcomed and enjoyed teaching, though it made us more than ever aware of our particular problem concerning the children's imaginative powers and possibilities. It is perfectly possible to teach *The Tale of Two Cities* or *The Kon-Tiki Expedition* in a way which enables a pupil of normal intelligence, or even a pupil of below average intelligence, to pass his Literature examination; but the pupil's examination result in no way indicates what is the nature of the 'meaning' these books have had for him. This point is discussed more fully in General Conclusions, pp. 172-3.

It can, of course, be argued that the same thing holds for English children who pass their examinations in England. This is so, but we felt there was a difference in kind rather than degree, which would merit much more careful following up of successful African candidates.

I have here dealt with prose only, as poetry and drama will be dealt with separately under their own headings.

2

WRITTEN WORK

(i) BASIC DIFFICULTIES

The following quotation is taken from a pamphlet issued by the Ministry of Education in the U.K.

> The problem of written composition will be less difficult if those of reading have been solved or are being solved. But composition has its own special difficulties in even the most favourable conditions.
>
> It was suggested . . . that composition ought to be the central written exercise in the English programme of all secondary schools. It is odd that this should need to be stated, but, in fact, a good many other exercises often oust composition. In grammar schools, for instance, the excessive use of "essays" in the full old-fashioned sense of the word[1] has done a great deal of harm, and it is only now coming to be recognised that this is a form of composition to be used very sparingly with the younger pupils. In many secondary modern and some secondary technical schools the situation is no better, since unsuitable essays appear there also; in schools free from essays the time has often been surrendered to manuals of composition consisting of little more than rather trivial verbal puzzles. Again, grammatical exercises are often overdone or badly done and in either case consume more time than they should; conversely, time is wasted because no grammatical terms are known at all. Finally, some of the topics treated, in modern technical and grammar schools alike, are remote from the pupils' lives and interests and arouse little urge to improve or to excel. In these circumstances the teaching of written composition makes little headway . . .[2]

We were fully in sympathy with these recommendations and criticisms and decided that whatever the difficulties, we must introduce original prose writing from the beginning in the entry class (Junior Secondary One).

[1] That is the artificial essay consisting of introduction, three paragraphs and conclusion.

[2] Ministry of Education Pamphlet No. 26. *Language. Some Suggestions for Teachers of English and Others.* Ch. 6 (1955).

As the whole concept of writing original continuous prose was foreign to the pupils, the first compositions were entirely guided by the teacher. This sounds as if we were not doing what we had set out to do; but if a child has never done a thing before, he must first understand what the teacher is asking him to do, and secondly he has to be shown how to set about it. It may seem an unbelievably basic thing to have to teach, but owing to the type of written work (if there had been any) previously practised—conscientiously practised by teachers conscientiously trained—hardly a child was familiar with the look or shape of a paragraph of continuous *written* prose, as opposed to printed prose. If they had written anything connected at all before coming to us, it had usually been in the shape of numbered sentences written underneath each other. Hence they were familiar only with perpendicular prose, and had never indulged in the horizontal variety. I know this to my cost, and would like to pause for a moment to consider its significance.

In 1957 I was teaching in an African Primary School and suffered from a rather narrow blackboard in the Primary V classroom. Having at last got the children to start writing connected sentences next door to each other instead of beneath each other, I then had the greatest difficulty in persuading them not to imitate *literally* what the narrowness of the board compelled me to write. For example, if I wrote as follows on the board:

Myself
My name is Betty
Mukasa. I am
eleven years old.
I live in a big
house near the school,
etc.

then this is exactly what appeared on the page of the exercise books of about half the class. When I pointed out (in Luganda) that they could write more than three words to a line in their exercise books whereas I could not write more than three words to a line on the board (demonstrating this), it never seemed to affect more than two or three pupils; the rest continued to copy as before. Sometimes, with great cunning I managed to write five words in one line on the board, but the three-word pupils continued to write in lines of three words in their books, though not necessarily consistently so.[1] Bearing in mind that this was neither stupidity nor malice, it would appear to be one symptom of the tremendous adjustment which has to be made by many African children to the mere phenomenon of writing. The written word is after all a very new thing in Uganda; its life-story is only just over fifty years old and there are still relatively few 'second generation' children in the schools. The inheritors of the first phonetic alphabet have had well over three thousand years to familiarize themselves with it. It is not merely the physical act of writing which is new, but lack of familiarity with the appearance of the written word. This is because the children come mostly from homes where the only form of hand-writing seen is probably in letters of a very elementary kind, and these would not necessarily be shown to the children. The printed word is more likely to have been encountered than the written word, in the shape of the vernacular newspaper and, for town children, in advertisements and notices.

The children who most readily adjusted themselves to 'horizontal prose' seemed to be those who had parents who had enjoyed some formal education, or else children from illiterate homes in villages or towns who were above average intelligence. The average child from an illiterate home had the worst struggle (leaving out children from homes of special difficulty), or perhaps I had not found a way of getting across to him the 'idea' or 'point' of writing in that particular way. I am certain that the most important and helpful thing for children learning

[1] I am aware that this kind of thing is often lightly dismissed as 'lack of concentration'. This does come into it, but it is not the kind of lack of concentration which accompanies 'lack of *attention*'. There is much more to it than this, and it deserves further investigation.

to write would be the introduction in the youngest classes of the communal class 'daily news wall-sheet'. This could then be followed by the personal 'daily news' or 'daily diary' book, written of course in the vernacular. This method has been well established as the basis of written work in the best of our Infant and Primary classes in England. Such a practice could be followed for two years, and re-introduced with the starting of the second language. This would help with the development of the 'connectedness of ideas', a more formidable problem than any visual one of form.

It may be as well at this point to emphasize the enormous importance to this development, of ideas of 'gradualness' and encouragement and imaginative sympathy on the part of the teacher. One of the main factors governing development is maturity, and nothing could be more repressive and less likely to produce the results desired than an unimaginative sergeant-major attitude on the part of the teacher. The young and immature are inconsequential, easily distracted, and, to the sophisticated adult, part of the charm of young children's work lies in its freshness and spontaneity of expression. A teacher can do irreparable damage by curbing this spontaneity in an attempt to force the child's development. If, for example, logical sequences of thought are demanded too prematurely, the child, not understanding what is being asked of him and unable to comply with his teacher's demands, often becomes frightened and ceases to be spontaneous. This leads to that lack of integrity which results from the fear of expressing one's own thoughts in one's own way, and to the adoption of second-hand ready-made ideas, partly, and often unconsciously, in propitiation of authority. On the other hand it can also lead to resentment and rebellion, as well as to other more complex manifestations. Many adults, such as the teachers one meets at Refresher Courses, when asked to participate in some exercise in producing original work, remark anxiously 'I'm no good at this'. This betrays the scars of the wounds inflicted by the unimaginative teacher with the punitive attitude, who pontificates about the 'discipline' of 'proper essay writing'. The first thing is to make a child feel that he can put down *fearlessly* what he thinks and feels about life around him. This will encourage him to gain that self-respect which is the basis of respect for others and also for their particular forms of expression.

Since there can be no original work without previous imitation (however paradoxical this may at first appear), it is essential that in the beginning the teacher should build up with the children a model of what is required, in accordance with the sentence structure (or 'patterns') already mastered by the pupils. (The simplest form of sentence is the simple main sentence; therefore the simplest paragraph of written prose consists of simple main sentences.) The class 'daily news' sheet in English Infant schools serves as a model for the subsequent (or contemporaneous) personal 'daily news' books, individual to each member of the class. In the entry class our guided compositions served as models for, or as an introduction to, subsequent written work. After about one term, they were no longer necessary.

I revived the practice of 'models' when the School Certificate class was first faced with the 400–500 word School Certificate 'essay'. When the class attempted the first two School Certificate subjects from an actual paper, I sat down with them and wrote the same essay. We then discussed its shape and length, and I typed it out and put it on the board so that they could see *what it looked like*, and get a kind of bird's eye view of it. I remember how dearly I had longed for something of the kind when I was preparing for the examination myself. Anyway this served its purpose, and thereafter pupils embarked on their School Certificate compositions with the confidence of visual familiarity with the form.

Our approach to form began then, very basically, by helping the children to write, first under the guidance of the teacher, then as soon as this was no longer necessary freely on their own, a reasonably coherent paragraph on a given subject. At all stages the written work was preceded by oral preparation. This consisted of discussion of the subject, vocabulary and idioms, and later, when we had found suitable models for some of the subjects, the reading aloud of the model. As the children's compositions grew from half a page to a page and gradually extended, it became natural to introduce sections (that is, paragraphs). For instance, during the first year the children found they could write a page to a page and a half on the subject, 'A Portrait of My Mother'. It was not too difficult to explain that this might be divided into two sections, one section being concerned with the description of the physical appearance of their mother, and the other section being concerned with her character and activities. Beginnings and endings were always discussed, and we always read out to the class the best attempts, the best beginnings and endings, and other passages illustrating certain points. By this means a concept and standard was built up to which everyone contributed. These constituted our immediate and short-term elementary problems, but we then had to think more deeply concerning (*a*) our long-term policy, and (*b*) what kind of writing we hoped to be able to develop.

(ii) APPROACH TO SUBJECT-MATTER

There are two kinds of prose; they are, I think, the only two possible kinds of prose, and one is good prose, the other bad prose. I do not pretend that the solidity of what I am calling good prose is always possible to sustain, or indeed, necessary to sustain. We must admit a *prose of expediency*; counters are legitimate as tokens of exchange when what we want is not truth, or beauty, but the vague generalizations that suffice us for the ordinary business of life. *But the prose of expediency is not the prose of art*; and even exact utilitarian or scientific prose is only good to the degree in which it is salted with the *vital imagery* and *an emotional content.*[1] [My italics.]

The written work we were going to try to develop would necessarily include the 'prose of expediency' (that is, strictly functional prose, which in everyday life is usually oral and

[1] Herbert Read, essay on 'English Prose' in *A Coat of Many Colours*, p. 93 (1945).

focused around our daily activities, cooking, working, shopping, visiting neighbours and so on), and also the 'prose of art', the latter being, of course, written. It was no part of our plan to develop one at the expense of the other. We were fully aware that if we were to help African children with their English our feet must remain on the ground—but on African ground. But we were equally aware that if we confined ourselves to the prose of expediency and neglected the prose of art we should be betraying our responsibility and depriving African children of one of their most desperately needed opportunities—that of developing their own creative imaginative powers. The development of civilization is surely also the development of consciousness, and to further this end the prose of art could be of inestimable value.

The prose of art (that is, the prose of reflection, of imagination; the written word) was to contain the heart of our teaching. The prose of art was an aim. We were under no illusions as to how difficult, or perhaps even impossible, it might be to achieve this aim. We had much against us and we felt profoundly our own ignorance.

For hours my young colleague and I brooded over the preparation and follow-up of our lessons, analysing the children's written work. We examined spelling, structures, words and idioms which had a special attraction for African children, words and idioms attractive to European children but apparently not meaningful to African children, appeals of different kinds of subject matter and the possible reason for this, and so on. We discussed and compared the reactions of the children in class, both in their oral work and in their general 'deportment', that is, ease, tension, hostility, mere superficial obligingness and so on.

We read and re-read Helen Keller:

'I was keenly delighted when I felt the fragments of the broken doll at my feet. Neither sorrow nor regret followed my passionate outburst. *I had not loved the doll. In the still dark world in which I lived there was no strong sentiment or tenderness*' . . . *This thought, if a wordless sensation may be called a thought,* made me hop and skip with pleasure. ... 'That *living word* awakened my soul, gave it light, hope, joy, set it free! There were barriers still, it is true, but barriers that could in time be swept away.[1] [My italics.]

In a world of strictly limited vocabulary, interests, experiences and imagery, and of partly ritually prescribed emotion, how much 'thought' could there be? What could we reasonably expect as a starting-point? How many of our pupils lived, part of the time at least, in a world of 'wordless sensation', and how were we to find the key to introduce to them the 'living word' charged with meaning and with vision? We hoped for vision and we hoped that we might not fail in compassion.

Before going to Uganda, and during the time when I had to take many demonstration classes of how to introduce and teach original composition to English children, I had had to face the peculiarly European urban problem of how to get at the original human being, now overlaid with a crust of advertisements, comics, cinema and television; and how to get that human being to express what he thought and felt, rather than what the advertisements, comics, cinema, and television had told him he thought and felt. A rather remote and innocent awareness of this problem is expressed in the following extract.[2]

As was suggested earlier, unsuitable practice includes not only stilted essays too early but also fanciful inventive narrative too often. This latter produces for the most part nothing more than the clichés and the stock situations of boys' magazines; in any case, the 'story' is too unmanageable to give much training in selection or form except to the naturally gifted story-teller, who is rare among pupils of school age. It does everybody good from time to time to let himself go, but the educational results of this occasional release ought not to be over-rated.

Working in our particular district of London, we did not encounter the clichés and stock situations of the boys' magazines

[1] Helen Keller, *The Story of My Life*, p. 28 (1947).

[2] Ministry of Education Pamphlet No. 26. *Language, Some Suggestions for Teachers of English and Others*, Ch. 6, p. 72 (1955).

in the 'fanciful inventive narrative' set by some well-intentioned visiting teacher who had temporarily descended from the grammar school sphere. (The favourite form of this sort of 'subject' was a stimulating sentence left thrillingly unfinished; for example, 'Betty and Jimmy were taking a Christmas parcel to their Grand-mother. They were walking through the wood when suddenly they heard a groan . . . .'.) What we inherited from such exercises were the unprintable clichés of what the children themselves cheerfully referred to as 'the hot-sex stuff' of the literature they bought under Waterloo Bridge. Dr Frederic Werthem, the psychologist, has analysed the influences of this type of literature on American children.[1] This problem would clearly not be solved by expurgated editions of English classics tenderly introduced into the Secondary Modern schools by the well-meaning believers in the equality of all human beings (using the word 'equality' as a synonym for 'sameness'). Nor, indeed, would it be solved by the doctrine—usually accepted as being more 'down-to-earth' and robust, not to say 'modern' and 'progressive'—of bringing the children's own choice, that is, comics, etc., into the classroom and extending it to detective fiction to show how 'matey' teacher really was. The supporters of this doctrine always laid stress on the spontaneity of the children's choice, though they left uninvestigated what the actual 'choice' consisted of. In the event of a choice between *A* and *B*, there being no *C* or *D*, and supposing *A* to be *Ivanhoe* or *David Copperfield* or *Vanity Fair* and *B* to be *Guys with Guns*, or *Murder in the Underground* or *She Did It Again*, and supposing the chooser to be living in East St, S.E.5, then 'spontaneous' is not a particularly illuminating or fitting epithet to describe the choice involved.

At that time I made a list of the forms of the prose of art. Bearing in mind man's urge to leave a record of his doings to posterity, we considered that the first art form to appeal to children might be the 'diary', that intensely personal record

[1] Dr. F. Werthem, *The Seduction of the Innocent.*

of an individual human being's activities; then letters, autobiography, and travel literature or any literature embodying personal experiences. This was all intensely subjective literature, written in the first person. It was 'true', and in all this type of writing first things came first, that is, the qualities that make for style (meaning ways of expression) rather than form. Sincerity, directness, simplicity, clarity, integrity, idiom, imagery, all could be encouraged and expressed within these art forms, whose very looseness and fluidity were especially suited to children of school age.

Real appreciation of form is a very mature quality, and can only be brought about by gradual development. The first step is to get the pupil to express what he has to say. Those who curb this written expression by trying to impose formal essays too early,[1] may well be putting the last nail in the lid of the coffin in which his imaginative potentialities are henceforth entombed. Those who uphold the 'discipline of the formal essay', at the other end of the scale, frequently set the 'fanciful inventive narrative' subject (also referred to in the Ministry of Education report).[2] This is not as paradoxical as it may seem, since the fanciful is precisely what the unimaginative understand by imagination.

While deciding that the subjective art-forms were the ones to embark on first, I had also made a rough list of the objective forms, to see what might serve our purpose there. I had listed biography, legends, folk-tales, short stories, adventure stories, the full-length novel, certain types of travel literature, and the literary essay not written in the first person. Later on we did in fact use some of these in our scheme.

In London I had found the subjective forms had had a profound appeal, but there was one other factor that had greatly and significantly contributed to the impact made by these prose forms: the influence of the model which had sup-

[1] This is, in fact, the 'stilted essay too early', referred to in the Ministry of Education Pamphlet.

[2] Ministry of Education Pamphlet, *op. cit.*

plied that sense of security so badly needed by a child embarking on something of his own, especially when he is not used to it. Part of the influence of the comics seen in children's writings is due, not just to the appeal of the subject matter, but to the need to imitate, the need to have something on which to base one's own efforts; if nothing comprehensible or appealing and, above all, manageable, is produced as a model, the child will find his own model.

I had gradually built up a selection of subjects with models attached, which I had tried out on a variety of occasions in a variety of situations.

Subject	*Model*
A page out of my diary	Extracts from the diaries of Elizabeth Fry and others
A page or chapter out of my autobiography	Carefully selected extracts from Noel Coward's *Present Indicative*
	Extracts from Laura Knight's *Oil-Paint and Grease-Paint*, vol. I
or	
My most vivid childhood memories (This was once set in a School Certificate paper.)	The extract about being frightened of going to bed in Julian Green's *Memories of Happy Days*, Ch. VIII
The empty house	Extract from Mary Webb's *Gone to Earth*, describing Undern, Ch. XXVI
Street market	D. H. Lawrence, *Sea and Sardinia*, various extracts
An incident on a journey	D. H. Lawrence, *Sea and Sardinia*, the description of the gossipy wife left behind on the journey to Mandas
My favourite dish	Discussion only
Things I have loved	Rupert Brooke, 'The Great Lover'

All these subjects were naturally approached first through discussion. It was then pointed out that famous writers and well-known persons had also thought upon these subjects and some had had rather nice things to say about them. The model was then produced, and read and discussed. I generally told the class something about the person who had written the passage. More often than not they asked me about the writer before I had time to start telling them about him. This indicated that the passage had touched them sufficiently for them to be curious to know more about the author. This method never once failed to gain their attention and interest, and when the suggestion was made that they should now suppose themselves in the place of the writer and say what they thought and felt about the subject, there was unhesitating co-operation. This procedure successfully removed from their writings all vestiges of comics and the like.

I have attributed the results of the method to the following causes:

(1) the subject-matter was within the actual experience or imaginative participation of every member of the class;

(2) the model did three things:

(*a*) it gave the pupils the security and confidence of knowing the kind of thing that they were being asked to attempt, and therefore unconsciously set a standard to be imitated (that is, an unconscious counterblast to the comics);

(*b*) it was in contemporary English and selected, for its evocative language, idioms, imagery and situations;

(*c*) it was written by writers either alive or recently dead with whose personal lives and ambitions the children could feel sympathy and identification.

Had I not had this previous struggle in finding a way to get very hard-boiled city products to write genuine original composition, I might never have had the temerity to try and find a way to get African children, so far removed from the

English city children, to attempt original imaginative composition.

I felt that the approach which had served me so well in a tough corner in England might somehow be adjusted and adapted to fit the situation in Uganda. You can do nothing with children until you have touched them, and I could not help feeling that something which had seemed to touch so many in England must somehow have some kind of universal validity.

The first thing was to think of subjects, then to find suitable models. The difficulties were formidable. One of my most successful subjects in England, 'The empty house', was completely useless in Uganda where the 'huts' or houses are of far too temporary a nature to have 'atmosphere' attached to them. African life is lived largely out of doors. Not enough of it is lived inside to build up in African children that infinite store of images, impressions and associations that a European child has in connection with the inside of a house which is his home. None of our African pupils had played among deserted ruins on a moonlight night to be startled suddenly by a shadow flitting across the surviving black wall of a bombed building; or had stumbled across an old shoe and perhaps asked himself the question, 'Whose was this, and when was it last worn?' No creaking cupboard door, askew on failing hinges, spoke of 'old unhappy, far-off things', or evoked the spirits of those that had lived there. The whole idea of the 'personality' of empty houses, the imprint left by those who have lived in them, was out of the world of African children. The model would arouse in them nothing meaningful, neither from the point of view of imagery nor emotion. Considering the animistic world that our African pupils inhabited, this statement may seem absurd. But when a European child peoples his environment with the forces of good and evil, he is at least partly conscious of the fact that he is doing so. European children are continually being reminded by their parents that they live in a world of 'common sense', information which, in certain circumstances, they do not always entirely believe. An African child with an animist background does not *consciously* people his world with good and evil spirits, for him it *is* peopled, and his parents' views confirm his own. In many cases, largely through schools, these beliefs have been driven underground by a cold douche of scorn from African teachers and others who have been affected by Western education, and African schoolchildren are careful not to express them. Nevertheless, one is continually coming across signs of their reality in the lives of those who are doing their best to suppress them. For example, a boy in Junior Secondary I, describing his grandfather, wrote,

He is a very clever man. He is a doctor. He cures many people by giving them medicine. Sometimes he poisons them too.

..Not even the extremely popular subject (in England) of 'My favourite dish' would have the appeal necessary to produce a piece of imaginative writing; for most African children did not, as far as we could gauge at that time, approach their food from any aesthetic point of view. The blue check cloth with splashes of sunlight on it, the bunch of yellow roses on the table did not enhance the enchantment of a fragrant dish of strawberries and cream, and at the end of three years of preaching on the virtues of African flowers, I still could not persuade our pupils to fill the jars I had provided for their dining-room tables. The snug kitchen with firelight on the wall, the kettle on the hob, the cat on Grand-dad's cushion and the delicious aroma of bacon sizzling in the pan, were equally outside their scope. They were shocked when told that many Europeans live and eat in their kitchens, for most local African kitchens are separate huts, uncomfortable, smoky, and draughty with a few bricks or stones to cook on and with earthen floors. Also, for many Africans, eating is bound up with ritual, with which we in our turn were unfamiliar.

Nevertheless I felt sure that the clue was to be found somewhere in the autobiographical approach. Perhaps no writer has stated the truth that all living organisms, including man, are egocentric, more endearingly and affectionately than Anatole France. 'Elle était toute petite, ma vie, mais c'était une vie, c'est à dire le centre des choses, le milieu du monde. Ne souriez pas à ce que je dis là, ou n'y souriez que par amitié et songez-y; quiconque vit, fut-il petit chien, est au milieu des choses.[1]

The trouble was that we did not know enough about the intimate details of the daily lives of our pupils.

(iii) BEGINNINGS OF ORIGINAL PROSE

Meanwhile we had to be getting on with something and in the lowest classes we began the guided compositions, the first one being 'Myself, and my family'. This was meant to revise (*a*) the basic list of people the pupils ought to know and be able to spell; and (*b*) the basic sentence—the simple main sentence.

It also gave us ample opportunity for remedial teaching, enabling us to try to put across the meaning of the word 'family', as there is no equivalent to the European concept in Luganda or vice versa! With regard to spelling, the following are typical examples, 'yaas' (for 'years'), 'brather', 'borther' (for 'brother'), 'mather' (for 'mother'), 'sisistis' (for 'sisters'), 'leven', 'a laven', 'laven', (for 'eleven'), etc. These are typical of analogic spelling, the result of the 'ears before eyes' principle so often advocated by numbers of educationists and teachers of the English language in Uganda. What they overlook is that the 'ears before eyes' principle presupposes that what the ears hear is correct and pure pronunciation, and is followed up by skilled pronunciation exercises. African teachers have, very understandably, the utmost difficulty in pronouncing certain sounds in English, some of which, like the 'o' in 'mother' and the 'un' in 'punish', have no equivalents in Luganda; this

[1] A. France, *Le Livre de mon ami*, (Paris, 1885). (It was a tiny little life, my life, but it *was* a life, which is to say it was the core of things, the centre of the universe. Don't smile at what I've just said, or if you do, don't smile unless with affection, and remember, whoever lives, even if only a little puppy-dog, feels himself to be the core of things.)

is, especially true of the 'ir' or 'ur' in 'bird' or 'burst'. In itself this is not a matter of great importance, but if the principle 'ears before eyes' is to be made the basis of the English teaching for the beginners—always taught by African teachers—it assumes an unnecessary importance. If what the ears hear is faulty pronunciation and enunciation it does not matter, providing the eyes have first or contemporaneously registered the visual image of the word correctly, helped by kinaesthetic experience of writing the word. If you say 'mather' but write 'mother' it may not be ideal but it is a sound basis for further development, and also for examinations which are vitally important to Africans. Moreover no-one will fail to understand you orally. On the other hand if you say 'mather' and write 'mather' it becomes a good deal more serious, from every point of view. Some of these faulty analogic spellings ('had' for 'heard' in particular) are never eradicated and persist to school certificate level.[1] If Sir Winston Churchill makes a speech in French in an accent which unmistakably betrays his origins, he will lose nothing in prestige or esteem, but if he writes a letter to the French Ambassador, which has every third word misspelt, and which shows his ignorance of the formulas of letter-writing in French, he will be judged illiterate as well as impolite. Presumably European educators in Africa should be aiming at developing educated Africans, not mere talkers who have remained basically illiterate, unable to express themselves in the written word, as a result of a crude system of instruction.

An additional difficulty for African teachers is that when in their own language every word ends in a vowel, there is frequent elision.

We first battled to get the new recruits in Junior I, to begin at the beginning of their exercise books, and not at the back and upside-down or in the middle, and persuaded them to write

[1] It should also be noted that once the link of the faulty sound has been established with the incorrect visual image (due to analogic spelling), all additional words containing the same sound are almost invariably similarly misspelt, for example panish, bandle, abandant, antil, straggle, trable, etc.

their names on the front and not the back; and to begin at the top of the page, not on the second line or lower down. We got them to co-operate in writing horizontal instead of perpendicular prose, and then had to start a major campaign against the fatuous use of the present continuous tense.

I invented a composition 'Laying the Table' to counterblast this. I brought the most attractive things I could find, a coloured striped table-cloth, a vase of flowers (revising and extending the names of colours, adding 'spotted, striped, checked, patterned'), coloured crockery, a blue enamel teapot and so on. The African children were keenly interested in what Europeans really have on their tables, in their rooms and houses, and they were anxious to know what was *comme il faut*, so that there was never any lack of interest or volunteers to come out and demonstrate the order of doing things. Nevertheless, we had a hard task to persuade them to substitute 'When I lay the table, I first put a red and blue striped table-cloth on the table. Then I put a vase of flowers in the middle of the table' etc., for the senseless but conscientiously drilled and learnt continuous tense, 'When I lay the table I am first putting a vase of flowers, etc.' The degree and extent to which the present continuous tense was ingrained, unrelated to any meaningful situation, can be seen from the fact that the prefixing of the subordinate clause 'When I lay the table' in no way affected the conditioned reflex of the drilled tense.

Together with the exasperating and wasteful business of eliminating errors which need never have been taught, came more interesting problems. Naturally we were trying to foster and develop (but not force artificially) a sense of sequence in both oral and written work. I set the third year class the composition 'Getting ready for school'. I was still fighting the present continuous tense, and I hoped to correct the wrong use of 'put on', 'wear', 'take off', 'dress' (that is, 'I am putting on my green dress on Mondays', for 'I wear my green dress on Mondays'); also the wrong use of 'boil' or 'cook' for making tea (that is, 'I cook the tea,' or 'I boil the tea' for 'I make the tea', or 'I boil the water for tea'). The latter is largely due to the fact that many Baganda do not possess the luxury of a kettle or tea-pot, and therefore a common procedure for tea-making is to boil water in a saucepan and then to sprinkle tea-leaves on the top, leaving this to brew a bit. To a European the result is merely coloured water, as not many tea-leaves are put in. Many African children in Uganda are brought up in surroundings which contain tea-plantations and are therefore acquainted with the green leaves of tea-bushes. Perhaps they think of the dried tea in terms of leaves, and therefore only refer to the actual liquid as 'tea'. In any case, where we should say 'Put the tea in the pot', or 'Where is the tea?,' many African children say 'Put the tea-leaves in the pot', or 'Where are the tea-leaves?' However, in this composition I was faced with a new and unsuspected problem with regard to sequence. The composition had been carefully prepared orally, largely on the question and answer basis, for example, 'When you wake up in the morning, Ssali, what do you do?' etc. I had based these questions in the first instance on my knowledge of what the sequence of actions would be for a European child from a simple home, and secondly on what I imagined an African child did before setting off for school. When I was correcting the written versions, which were of good quality, two changes in the sequence had taken place, except in the books of the rather more comfortably-off boys.

The changes were as follows:

Oral preparation

(*a*) During the oral preparation I had stressed the practicalness of putting the kettle or saucepan on as soon as the fire was lit so that there would be no waste of time, and the water would be getting hot while the pupils washed and dressed.

(*b*) After drinking the tea and clearing up the tea-things, the bicycle would be *fetched*, school-bag hung on the handle-bars and the pupil would set off for school. (Some boys did not make tea, but ate the left-overs from the night before.)

Changes

(*a*) The pupil got up, lit the fire and waited for the water to boil.

(*b*) After drinking the tea and clearing up he got dressed, *took* his bicycle and books, washed his feet and set off for school.

This led me to some sober reflection before I checked my conclusions with the authors.

(*a*) I could not satisfactorily explain this change.

(*b*) Remembering the great care the children take of their school uniform, and realizing that most of them have only one, it was then clear to me that they would not put on their white shirt and shorts till the dirty jobs had been done. Three questions then arose: (1) Did they wear a night-shirt?; (2) Did they go about naked in the hut? Older boys have their own huts. I did not know enough about Baganda customs; (3) Did they put on some ancient shirt or garment till ready to go to school?

A point worth noting here is that these definite departures from the oral preparation would never have occurred, and hence I should never have been aware of the problem, if we had not encouraged the pupils from the beginning to be fearless and honest about themselves, their customs and attitudes, and convinced them of our sincerity in this.

As for washing their feet last, where would the water be? Outside of course, so that it was in fact much more sensible to wash your feet last, with your bicycle beside you, and then leap on to the bicycle with clean feet.

Why did they substitute 'took' for 'fetched'? With my European mind, and inability to imagine myself in the position of the African child, I had pictured fetching the bicycle from a shed or some vague place outside. Had I pondered the matter properly and remembered that school-boys are not infrequently attacked by gangs for their bicycles, and remembered also the glimpses I had had inside African houses, I should have realized that the bicycle is, of course, kept in the house with its owner, though not even this precaution is always effective against burglary.

I checked on these points in class, and they were confirmed with kindly amusement. Most children put on some old thing till the moment came for them to don their uniforms, and washed their feet last in the yard. There remained (*a*), which still rather mystified me. Then a boy of very poor parents, who lived in a hut of his own construction under the supervision of some remote relative, explained that it would be useless to light the fire and leave it, as the wood was rarely of a quality and quantity to ensure the continued vitality of the fire. It needed constant tending, and he certainly couldn't get dressed till afterwards.

The wealthier boys boiled their water on Primuses, so that the orally prepared sequence did not disturb them.

Had a composition, set in the School Certificate examination, involved a sequence such as this, it would not be impossible for an examiner, even one acquainted with Africa, to penalize a candidate for apparent incoherence, whereas the sequence had been written down literally as it occurred in daily life.

As our aim was to extend the children's imaginative participation by all the means at our disposal, we watched very carefully for the possible interrelation between one creative activity and another—not that we had reached the creative stage in English at that point. Nevertheless we soon realized that there was a noticeable inter-action between the painting and English lessons. For instance, in the painting lessons we were at first confronted with what seemed to us an extraordinary situation where the children apparently had no proper powers of recognizing certain colours for which they had no word in the vernacular.[1] Consequently teaching the names, and recognition of colours, was one of the first things which the activity of painting involved, and this had its repercussions in such exercises in English as the one already mentioned, 'Laying the table'. As we continued extending the pupils' vocabulary in the art room, this aroused a new interest and pride in showing off their accomplishment in the English lessons. We then set about timing certain written work in English to fit in with

[1] cf. ch. 5, 'Painting'.

parallel activity in the art lessons. So it came about, though not in as organized a way as it may seem on paper, that we timed our first portrait in the art room to coincide with the composition, 'Portrait of my Mother' in the English lesson. I think it was this combined exercise which first gave us a glimpse of what might develop. The pupils came to the English lesson primed with the vocabulary gained in the painting lesson, and, even more important, with what appeared to be a new way of looking at people.[1] When it was suggested that you could produce a 'picture' of a person using words instead of shapes and colours, and this was what writers, as opposed to painters, did, the quality of the interest aroused struck us as being different from what we had experienced before. Moreover it began to be flavoured with humour, the quality which more than any other is inseparable from language and through it largely governs people's conception of the comic. I realise that this evaluation of the quality of the children's interest is subjective, but a less subjective type of evidence was to be found in the written work resulting from this oral preparation. There, the level of achievement in fluency and accuracy, as well as to the kind of feeling or reaction the children had attempted to express (in a very groping, tentative way, as this was not a guided composition), did indicate that their interest and imagination had been more deeply involved than before.

In the preparation for this composition, 'Portrait of my Mother', we tried to put across the following points:

(1) Africans are not black (any more than Europeans are 'white').[2] They are anything but that, from those with honey-coloured skins or those glowing with deep gold, to the rich black-currant or plum-coloured ones. In the classroom the analogy of 'black-currant' or 'plum' was no good, of course, and instead we used the grenadilla and the colour of egg-plant for comparison. This led to the discovery that many of the children did not 'know' these—at least this is what they said.

[1] cf. ch. 5, 'Painting'.

[2] cf. ch. 5, 'Painting'. *ibid*

I do not mean they merely did not know the English words for them, because when those who knew the Luganda for them tried to explain what they were, they met with no success. They seemed not to have 'registered' them, although they are to be seen in nearly every market, whether in towns or country. We planned our composition, 'A visit to the market', as a result of this.

We pointed out that a painter or writer's admiration would naturally be aroused by the contemplation of African colouring, and the rich variety of skin colours would be a challenge to his ability to find suitable expression for it. We also said that we realized that we ourselves, in the eyes of Africans, must resemble what we felt to be the unstimulating pallidness of a peeled banana. This evoked expressions of amused surprise.

We had not anticipated the effect of this little discussion. The children's attention was wholly arrested, and smiles spread over every face, though some expressed a kind of puzzled incredulity at the notion that the skin of an African might be considered of superior beauty and worth, in any circumstances. This particular response was infallibly elicited each year with each new set of pupils admitted to the school.

(2) The fascination of a portrait lies in the departure from a norm, and every living being is a departure from an ideal norm. Although everyone's face is a collection of the same features, no two people look exactly alike. Here I always gave a selection of outstanding characteristics I had observed in various pupils in the class; the unusually large space between the eyes and ears of one boy, for example, which made him interesting to look at and might predispose a portrait-painter to want to paint his portrait; the shape of the hair-line of another boy, which made a particularly attractive frame to his face, and so on. This increased surprise and amusement, and when I added that every human being was unique and unrepeatable, and said, 'There is only one of you, Paulo Mukasa, there has never been a you before, and there will never be another', this was received as an astonishing revelation, not

really believed by anyone, but exercising considerable fascination. I followed this up with the magic of science, pointing out that police detection of criminals relied to some extent on this uniqueness in the skin pattern of people's finger-tips and the pattern made by their marks. This made a more convincing impression, and the rest of the lesson was usually spent answering eager questions arising from it. Not infrequently some of the children had a relation or friend who had been obliged to leave his fingerprints in the files.

When dealing with the physical aspect of a portrait, I taught the word 'plump', a type of beauty much appreciated by the Africans; the word was never forgotten, and in my spelling-records I can only find one instance of the usual analogic misspelling, 'plamp'. I also pointed out the difference in people's ways of walking, and taught the words, 'dignified', 'majestically' and 'queenly' in connection with their long-robed women. We have already observed that all such words would be excluded on scientific grounds from the word-frequency lists. Nevertheless these were the words which our pupils seemed to remember effortlessly, and subsequently employed most aptly; they were evidently charged with an appeal and evocativeness, emotional or otherwise, ignored by compilers of word-frequency vocabularies. The following quotation, therefore, is relevant. It is from Dr. Michael West's 'Explanation' at the beginning of his dictionary, *A General Service List of English Words*. The quotation (on p. viii) is as follows:

The chief values of the list are that it shows:

(1) how very heavy is the learning-burden of the major words compared with all the others, and how very much the learner's task may be lightened by cutting out everything which is not really essential, especially in those heavy words.

(2) how much less frequent and less important are the minor items of words than one would have expected. *Indeed it may be taken as a general rule that anything which seems in the least degree unusual or doubtful should certainly be excluded from the teaching course.* [My italics.]

This begs the questions, once more: 'Which teaching course, and for whom, and to what end?'

We deliberately used the written composition to extend the children's vocabulary and idioms, as idioms are inseparable from imagery.

It is quite an illusion to imagine that one adjusts oneself to reality without the use of language and that language is merely an incidental means of solving specific problems of communication or reflection. The fact of the matter is that the 'real world' is to a large extent unconsciously built up on the language habits of the group.... We see and hear and otherwise experience very largely as we do because the language habits of our community predispose certain choices of interpretation.[1]

Moreover idioms are in fact the 'salt' of prose.

The unit of good prose is either the image or the idiom. Good prose is a mosaic of these units arranged with some regard for rhythm, which is a physical quality, ensuring ease. The image is the closest verbal counterpart of the thing seen; a clean word, fitting closely like a glove, a word with no ragged edges of vagueness or indecision. Such words are placed in some illuminating relationship one with another.... Good prose ... depends not so much on new analogies as on stark visualization. The image is evoked by the bare relation. And it is this kind of prose that is most permanent in its appeal, since it involves no element of fancy and therefore no element of fashion ...

Images are the rudiments of a literary art, but ... there is another element ... This other quality which is added to the moments of imagery has for its unit the idiom. *An idiom is literally a way of expression peculiar to a person or a language. ... An idiom then becomes the unit of style: it is the outcome of those hereditary and environmental influences which determine in any man his individual predilections and fancies. It is an index to his personality.*[2] [My italics.]

As stated in chapter 1, our aim was to find this personal language for each African child we taught, and to develop in him his own vision and way of expressing it, that is his own 'style'.

[1] Edward Sapir, 'The Status of Linguistics as a Science', in *Language*, ch. 5, pp. 207–14 (1929).

[2] Herbert Read, essay on 'English Prose'. *Coat of Many Colours*, p. 93 (1945).

To give some idea of what we had to work on when the children arrived, examples are given below from their entrance examination. I had once misguidedly set the composition subject as follows: 'Write ten lines on "Myself and my Family".' Nearly all the answers were as follows: 'I think you are quite well. I think you have good family.' etc. I therefore learnt my lesson and the next year I set, 'Describe the Chief of your village'. (Write about half a page.)

(1) *A boy aged eleven* (He wrote 'eg 11')

Our chief is L. Mutayimbwa
Our chief has many doing
The chief have going to looking the pipils
The chief have happy with our pipils
The chief can help his pipils
The chief is very good man

(2) *A boy from another school, aged 13*

Describe the chife of my village.
I like my describe because I glad me.
when I am going our home I like me
he said, that if you come you can running.
he said when did you go school?
he going our village to see our man
Describe going Gombolola chife to do our works.
Gombolola chife he sadi describ go and tell you village

(3) *Another boy from the same school aged 12*

The Chief of My Village

My Chief's name is Mr. Lubowa.
He is a quite good leading parson.
He has a good house with taps of water inside
He is a brown man and his married man.
Two children one boy and one girl.
He has got a car.
And he always take me to school when he is going to his biseness.
His house is well smented and well painted it looks better.

(4) *A girl aged 14*

The chief of our village is very kind chief.

She is give us a good thing. and he give us able to works in our garden.

One day she go in our village to see their people and bring their things. she is like take some things to eat and dunk

When he go in the road he see a very big snake

She is like to beat of their things.

(5) *A girl from the same school aged 12*

The chief your name is Tomasi is very good man it is one woman and boy and girl He is many people in our village every day she works our chief.

The chief she is works everyday and go to Kampala every day I buy your market. The chief I live at Lugala.

The above examples illustrate the perpendicular prose and attempts at the horizontal variety, and there are several hundred of those before me as I write. It must be remembered that all candidates had had at least three years of English, and many had had four.

The English examination included an oral examination which naturally influenced us a good deal. Nevertheless it should be clear that (3) shows a better grasp of language and basic structure than the others, and also signs of what we were looking for—a spark of originality and evidence of imaginative power (for example, 'taps of water inside', 'well smented and well painted'). There is genuine observation and imaging here. There is the usual analogic spelling of 'parson' for 'person' and 'his' for 'he's'. There is also some sense of sequence; the chief is introduced as a leading person, then we learn he has a good house and is married, then that he has children and a car. Then we hear that he takes the writer to school on his way to work.

It is interesting to see how a boy of this potential is influenced by the literature read. This is shown in the following passage quoted without alteration, which he wrote nine months after being admitted to the school:

The Twelve Brothers

The girl took the twelve shirts and went on. She walked all day, and in the evening she saw a small boy who asked her where she was going. Benjamin said, 'What are you looking for, and where are you going?' 'I am the King's daughter and I am looking for my twelve brothers, and I shall go until to the end of the world.' Then she showed him the twelve shirts that belonged to her brothers. Benjamin new at once that she was his sister, and Benjamin said, 'I am Benjamin, your youngest brother.' And they all cried for happiness. 'But there is one thing that troubles me,' Said Benjamin. 'My eleven brothers and I had agreed to kill any girl we see because we were forced to leave our Kingdom and come to this forest because of a girl.'

'I shall willingly die in that way if I can help my brothers.' 'No, no, you will not be killed, you will hide in that small room until my brothers come back, and I will tell them about you.' . . .

It is also interesting to see how his individual qualities, which could be glimpsed in his entrance paper, have developed by the beginning of the second term in the second year. The following composition was in fact done in the first lesson of the second term, after six weeks' holiday, and is reproduced without correction:

A Portrait of my mother

First my mother is rather young. When she laughs very much fine lines come in her eyes and the eyes look soft too. She has rather big ears, with a pointed nose. Her lips are thin, and she has a smooth skin. Once I was down with fever and she came on my bed[1] and gave me a gentle smile and a loving one too. When she comes from the garden her hands are rough and horny but when she washes them they become again smooth. She has a brisk but majestic walk. She is good tempered.

Secondly when you do a bad thing in my mother's presence she tells you to do it in a good way. My mother is strict about anything which efects her children, and she tries to see that you do it in a good way. She is a hard-working lady and on Saturday she bustles the house like a polite soldiers suching for a thing in the house.[2]

Finally when she has finished working she gets a bath and put on her best dress and sit in the chair and do other work such as making

[1] Usually a mat on the floor.

[2] The Luganda word 'omuserikale' meaning soldier, is also used for 'policeman').

a mat, making a basket and making the table cloths. Once my little brother cried for nothing and my mother asked him why he was crying then he said nothing then my mother gave him a smacking on the head and he cried more. Because she hate crying for nothing thats why my mother beat him. When she goes to visit she puts on her Sunday dress.

This boy used to write quickly, and accuracy in original composition was apt to suffer, but the following passage taken from a composition 'A Visit to Kampala Post Office' illustrates still more clearly which elements in a situation appealed to him most strongly:

I walked out, but what surprised me is to see a lady who looked very smart and looked like a town-lady to ask me where she could put her letter to go to Bulemezi. Without a stamp! I asked her, 'I am willing to help you, but where is the money for the stamp?' She said to me, 'what? did you say a stamp, do you want to steel my money? only that small piece of paper they put on, do you buy it? Go away you little boy, I know boys in Kampala.' This of a woman who knows boys, and know nothing about posting a letter.

Here is another example from the entrance paper. A boy, aged 15, wrote

My chief is very great chief in my village. he likes all the people who lives in my village he works very hard. Because he like all the people in the village to be happy he don't like the thief or the men who want to kill another man to take theirs things he always sleep in very clean house He wants every man to have his garden He alway have a little walk and see what wrong in the village he go in the church in every sunday. He like to every man to have a lot of work. I like my chief very much.

This is a very quiet, gentle boy, whose yearning for peace and order, and desire that all men should be content and happy is often expressed in his written work in a curiously lyrical way.

The following composition was written nine months after entry:

In the Garden

On evening a man and his wife went in the garden It wasn't a long way from the house It was quite near. His wife took a box of biscuits and the man took only a packet of cigaretes with him. When they came there the wife said, 'This is a beautiful garden to look at. 'I also feel very happy,' said the man. Then the man picked a flower and gave it to her[1] wife this made his wife more happy and as hee husband walked a short distance the wife began to sing in swahili language. she also made her husband more happy. In that time they were full of happines the sun shone but not so hot, and the birds were singing sweetly for myself I think it was a nice day for them. After two hours they wanted to return back then the wife picked an armful of flowers for her house they came home hand in hand.

It will be seen that this example is the 'index' to a personality very different from that of the writer of the previous one, and couched in a very different idiom. It is of psychological significance that when this boy retold the story of Hansel and Gretel he made the wicked step-mother say to her husband, 'Don't worry, I will help you', whereas every other member of the class had some version of the original, expressing determination to get rid of the children and contempt for the father's hesitation. Even at this humble level we can see clearly the penetration of Herbert Read's observation,

As the events were received into each mould of sensibility, so the cast of those events which we evoke in writing emerges with all the sutures of this mould. Idiom is the sum of those influences which determine, not only our choice of words, but also their arrangement in a personally appealing rhythm. It is the expression of what Remy de Gourmont called the emotive memory; it is the element which joined to a visual memory determines style.[2]

It will be noted that this boy was over fifteen when admitted to Junior I. The difficulty of trying to get pupils to understand and include proper punctuation so late in their language-learning life is obvious. Ill-digested punctuation always comes to light in original writing which has any degree of spontaneity.

[1] There is no difference between the possessive adjectives 'his' and 'her' in Luganda. Further, possessive adjectives agree with the thing possessed not with the possessor.

[2] Herbert Read, essay on 'English Prose' in *A Coat of Many Colours*, p. 93 (1945).

The next example is taken from the entrance paper of a girl, aged 13. She came from a Mission school where there is considerable European influence and where the children are sometimes taught by Europeans. This probably accounts for the fact that her composition was written as a proper paragraph.

Composition

The name of my chief is Mukasa, he lives at Mabanda, he was very rich man. He has a Motor-car, he is a very good man because he teach us how to be clean. He has a very good house, he have ten acres of land, he is very kind man, he have ten dogs in his home. He was very long, he have one woman and two savents. He have a hoe and a good children. The name of his father is Mr: Mako. He was a very good man because he look-after the people which there on her village. Do you seen her? every day he came to Kampala to buy something.

A few months after being admitted into Junior I she wrote the following original composition:

When I was small

When I was small I used to help my mother to cook food, to fetch water from the well, to fetch wood from the little house, to fetch solt from the main house, to threw rubbish out side the banana garden. I would often help my father to plant flowers.

When I was out side the house I used to play with my cat and my little dog.

Some-times I play with my parrot. When it is raining I use to sing my beautiful songs and I play out side the house in water. When my mother was not there, I used to play with her knife, I pick frowers with it and I cut wood with it. Some-times she beats me, I would cry when my sister was at school and sometimes I used to go to school with her.

My father used to play with me, and he never beats me whatever happens, he cannot beat me, because I am the first girl in my family, he wants to leave me in my happiness.

There was a pond near our neighbour's house and we would swim in it with John he was the oldest son. When I was small I love him with my heart and now, he loves me too. My mother used to look-after the garden and sometimes I help her.

Note the examples of analogic spelling: 'solt' (c.f. 'olways' for 'always'), 'rabbish'; while 'frowers' illustrates the Luganda inter-changeability of 'r' and 'l'. The parrot appeared in a number of compositions at that time, because I owned one, and pupils who used to carry my books to the house for me could see the parrot on the veranda. I used to return occasionally to find pupil and parrot staring silently at each other in mutual fascination. The children could never understand how it was that the parrot 'talked'.

This girl's respect for cleanliness (she was extremely particular in the matter) is expressed in a way which shows the developing imagery and idiom we hoped to encourage. The extract is taken from 'A letter to my Teacher', written five months after her entry into the school. Having stated that she was alone at home, she then writes,

At two o'clock[1] I saw my friend walking in the road. Then when I saw her I was very happy indeed and I ran very quickly to meet her. Then I looked at her head, but her hair was very dirty and if you looked at her dress you couldn't eat.

I was particularly amused by this image, on account of its closeness to the German idiom '*Da vergeht einem ja das Essen*'. (The equivalent of 'It puts you off your food'.)

The following is taken from the entrance paper of a boy, aged 13. It was outstanding for its competence compared to the average standard. The few compositions, which were written in paragraph form, and not as sentences underneath each other, did in fact indicate a much better background. This was almost always borne out in the oral interview. There were a few exceptions, of course, but very few.

Composion about the Chief of my village

The Chief of my village is called Misaeri Lwanga. He has a very nice house. He has one wife and four children. That Chief is my

[1] All children had been taught to say 'p.m.' and 'a.m.' as this is how it was taught in their text-book. We had a great battle to correct this to the normal usage, and to convince the children that 'a.m.' and 'p.m.' was time-table language.

brother. He is very kind to every one, who goes to visit him. When you want to visit him. His house is beside Masaka road. His house is a big house with big windows. He has many cows. He has a new car. I went to visit him last Sunday. When some one fight the people catch thieves and take them in his prison.

This is the end of my composion.

After a few months in the school he wrote the following original composition:

When I was small

When I was young and small I did not go to school I would play a lot with friends and we used to play many games such as hiding, running, and telling lies each another. I used to sit on the back of a goat, the goat did not like me. It used to push me away with its head. I used to think that trees were alive and I used to talk to them funny things, I told them to sing to me and they answered nothing and I would beat them hard and I thought that they could cry. I used to cry as a chick as it cries when it is under its mother.

I did not want to work hard. My mother would tell me good stories, I and my friends used to clap when she ended the story. We used not know the use of going to school and I was much afraid of cows and wells.

I enjoyed my life when I was small.

By the middle of the second year there was no doubt that the starting-point of original, imaginative composition must be the autobiographical one, and that the centre of interest must, in the first instance, be the writer. Then the interest must be extended to the right of other human beings to be themselves. This approach bore fruit, when combined with the remedial teaching which gave the pupils the necessary grasp of simple language in which to express what they wanted to say. It was helped by all the other influences already mentioned—extension of sense experience, observation and awareness, and by the influence of the literature studied and the models read.

Examples are given below of the kind of observation we were getting in original work in the second year. There are two things to be kept in mind. First the children were being trained to look on human beings with a new eye. Secondly, whatever private observations the children may have made previously, they had not known that these observations were of worth or interest to anyone else. They were now beginning to realize that it was this truthfulness, combined with the writer's own individual way of expressing it, that interested *them* in the Literature they read. When now they asked, 'Is it true?' and we said, 'Not exactly. It is only "true" because the writer has seen this kind of thing happen, and has seen people behaving *like* this', their comment was, 'But it *seems* so true'.

The examples are all taken from a composition, 'A Bus Journey', The model had been the description of Emil's train journey in *Emil and the Detectives*, so that the children's interest had been directed to their fellow-passengers. In fact, when asked, 'Why is Emil's journey interesting to us to read about?', they found the answer was 'Because of the way in which the writer describes the other passengers and the way in which they think and feel about each other'.

The writers of the examples were boys, except where otherwise stated, and the average age was fourteen.

(1) [Referring to a group of Indian boys]: They were talking very loudly like birds on a tree. If you were outside the bus you might think that they were quarrelling.

The writer of the next extract (2) was a girl. She had eye trouble, and screwed her eyes up a good deal. I should like to emphasize again the immense importance to the children of knowing that no-one was *ever* allowed to laugh at anyone else's efforts in the classroom, or to ridicule anybody's weakness, whether physical or otherwise. This is important in England, but in an African school where children are particularly vulnerable, it must take priority over everything else, or fear may put an effective stop to any desirable development.

(2) A rude man asked, You girl, why have you got little eyes? Can you see very well? And why are you in poor clothes? you are looking very bad. You must have a pair of shoes. This man was very proud.

The children always came with the notion that 'proud' meant 'conceited' or 'vain'. There is one word for these concepts in Luganda and they had got hold of the wrong English translation. We used to have interesting discussions on the various forms of 'conceit'.

(3) [Describing a polite man] He had a pipe but he did not smoke it for he didn't want us to smell tobacco.

(4) [The writer of this one is a girl.] Mr, Kasasa was deaf, he gave many signs to us to make us understand what he meant, but unfortunately I did not understand anything. I just watched his signs but nothing entered my mind. In other ways he was good company, if he had not been deaf. His face was clean and his hair well-brushed. He washed his feet properly as well as his shirt and pair of shorts. Some people laughed at him when he made his signs, but I thought it was not good.

(5) He had no shoes on his feet but he had a beautiful watch on his wrist. He looked at it all the time. He seemed to be a thief because he did not want anybody to look in his eyes.

(6) She was black with a bright nose and had one eye always closed because it was not well. She moved her head with water coming from her bad eye and her eye made me sorry for her so that I advised her to go to Mulago hospital.

The children always called the very dark-skinned Africans, usually from Nyasaland and other territories, 'black', and they referred to the lighter-skinned people as 'brown' in much the same way as we use the adjective 'fair'.

(7) All her teeth were squeezed together.

(8) He looked as if his eyes were going to jump from him.

(9) He was a drunkard. After a short time he started vomiting in the carriage and the carriage was all smelling of beer. He had nine fingers. I feared him very much because I thought he was an animal.

The comment about the fingers means that he had lost one finger.

The next examples are by girls.

(10) [Describing an Acholi] He greeted me but I did not know his language so I just said 'm-m-m-m-m-m.' He had a very big stomach. He touched it several times. I think it hurt him because very often Acholi people eat food which is not cooked yet.

(11) She was wearing sandals which were very big to her, when she was walking to the driver telling him that it was her time to leave, one of her shoes stayed behind.

(12) [A child had broken a window in the bus. The writer then reports] The conductor said, 'Please, why do you not prevent your child from going to the window? Now do you see what has happened?' The woman, instead of asking him to forgive her, said, 'Because you haven't ever had a child that's why you say so'. I left them shouting and I went out.

The examples quoted above are instances of how their own experience, the bus journey, has been illumined by their experience of reading and discussing Emil's train journey.

It is interesting to compare with this their expression of the impact made by this reading. Examples are given below (second-year English).

(1) *Comments on Mr Green*

He knew how to read because he was reading a newspaper.

He was bright of skin but dark in heart.

Mr Green was not a gentleman because he told Emil foolish[1] stories and he was a thief.

He had an inquisitive nose.

(2) *Comments on Emil*

He wore a school cap and a pair of shoes. He was well-behaved.

Emil was in great need of sweets.

His face showed that he was educated.

There was a cap on Emil's head and he wore a tie.

Emil feared that the police would say, 'He is a painter of noses and statues'.

(3) *Comments on Mrs James*

She had shoes.

She was a lady because she did not shout at Mr Green when he was telling Emil foolish stories.

[1] This class had not yet been told the phrase 'tall stories'.

She had put on some small shoes which hurt her and then she took them off in the carriage. Perhaps they could not stand her weight.

She was waving her foot up and down to make it cool.

(4) *Comments on the woman making the baby's cap*

[This woman comes out best, because she corresponded to the children's ideal of the well-behaved, and, of course, docile woman.]

She was humble because she did not say anything.

This woman was very polite.

She was a lady because she didn't say anything.

She was quiet and humble.

The following extracts are taken from the composition, 'The teacher I liked best (or least) in my primary school':

(1) He was a wise teacher because he first read what he would teach the next day.

(2) But the one thing I saw which was bad about him was that he spoke behind other people's backs. Although I was only a pupil, I was very careful about him, so that he did not say about me when I knew his bad habit.

The expression 'behind people's backs' had greatly caught the fancy of the children. It had occurred a very long time before the above composition, in a completely different connection.

(3) She had a good voice, not the sort of voice which can frighten you.

(4) He used to tease us and make us look foolish. His wickedness even made the stones angry with him.

This is apparently influenced by the frog in the story of the frog-prince saying to the weeping Princess who had lost her ball, 'Your tears would make even the stones sorry for you'.

(5) When he wanted your men or anything he would first ask you before he took it.

(6) He said, 'I do not beat anyone, but the Examination will beat you'.

(7) He used to make us lift his motor-cycle so that it might not get dirty.

(8) He always used to stand up quickly, but he kept us standing for a long time, about ten or fifteen minutes, just standing without saying anything. So we thought him very unkind.

A further selection of extracts from the composition, 'The life-story of a shirt', illustrate how fresh a subject of this kind is when tackled by African children for whom it is entirely new. The teacher can, of course, learn a great deal from this freshness of approach, free from any preconceived ideas (second-year English).

(1) Here I am, an old shirt who wants to tell you the story of his life. I was made of cotton. The cotton came from Uganda in a big bale.

When I was in that bale I was in the form of good soft cotton without seeds. I was put on a train which carried me from Uganda to Mombassa. I was placed in the ship with many other bales of cotton. I came to know this when we were far out and heard the splashes of the water and felt the coldness. . . . Next morning he put me on and he looked nice. He wore me every day and after one and a half years I got torn at the back but I was still clean. He took me to a tailor to make a small shirt for his son. I was given to the son, but the son was very dirty and made me dirty too. I was put into a nice suitase with good smells. Although I was dirty I was happy and my dirtiness was not queer. The son got fatter and fatter like a pig and now I don't fit him. I am in his suit-case until I will be given to another boy to whom I will fit perfectly.

(2) At first I was a seed. A man took me and sowed me in his garden. He always came to see me, and dug up some grass which was near me.

When I was old enough, about six months, he pulled me from my trees. He got all the rubbish which was on me and through it away.

(3) But when the Indian was cutting me with scissors I was like a man who is going to die. Because I have no life I did not die, only listened to the scissors . . . He sewed me with a machine, but the machine was very bad, it only jumped to me like a man who is trotting. . . . Then he threw me into a latrine until the germs ate me and I disappeared.

(4) [By a girl, aged fourteen and a half.] Once upon a time when I was not exactly a shirt, I was first a seed of cotton. The African

people started sowing me in their fields. . . . The tailor sewed me by machine and he finished me in a short time. The people who were in a [meaning 'the'] shop started calling, 'A shirt, a shirt, it is a beautiful shirt'.

(5) [By a girl, aged fourteen.] I came from London I think, I did not understand very well where I cam from because I was very young at the time, I think that I cam from London, because I know that is the place where the people make us, the person who told me that was the old piece of material which was lying near me. We were all in rolls. . . . He [the shop-keeper] pulled me down, put me on the table, then he measured me and cut me off. I cried very softly because he hurt me very much I cried, 'Cha-cha-cha-cha'. [imitating the noise of scissors] . . . The tailor put me on the machine and began to sew me, I cannot tell you how many tears I cried I think it may be that it was one potful. . . .

Finally I was torn into small pieces, and he threw me away. Then the rain came and washed me away into dirty places. I did not understand what was next because I was blinded by soil.

It is evident that what we have called 'imaginative participation' and 'imaginative sympathy' have been expressed in the examples quoted.

In case it is argued that this kind of imaginative expression is unusual, six more examples are given below from the *same* class, in which every single member did, in fact, show signs of it, in varying degrees.

(6) [By a boy, aged fifteen.] I was taken to a tailor he cut me out and sewed me by machine. I felt as if something was walking on me and tying me very hard.

(7) As I was very old and ragged, the man bought me for cleaning his car.

I cleaned it until I was thrown by the children into the field. I stayed in the field for about three weeks. When I was still there I heard the man asking his children whether they had seen me anywhere.

Their answer was no. I wanted to talk and to tell him where I was but it was difficult for me. When I was still living the white ants bit [he means 'ate'] me and changed me into soil. So my life stopped there.

(8) [By a boy aged thirteen and a half.] Then the man told my master to cut off two yards and those two yards were me. . . . The wife said, 'You buy clothes for yourself but you do not think of me although I work harder than you. Since I married you this is the third year and you have bought me only one cloth.[1] . . . and when time passed he threw me away full of germs, and then I was not known as a shirt which had been very beautiful. [The poignancy of this is peculiarly African.]

(9) [By a boy aged fourteen.] He came in the night drunk and he did not know that I was on the bed and when covering himself he threw me down on a very dirty floor. The time came for me to be worn and he put me on and went to work. The first day I was happy but the next day the days started to become worse and worse for he was a carrier and carried things on his back and I had to suffer all that trouble. . . . After a short time I was worn out but the man still wore me I saw people laughing. I thought to myself, 'I think they are laughing at me,' at that time I was not happy at all.

(10) [By a boy aged fifteen.] When we arrived at Liverpool in England they tied me up with my other friends. Small children of my friends were killed . . . Then I was taken to a tailor who was to make me into a shirt. He too took a scissors and began to cut me into small pieces I was afraid to this, to be like a piece of meat and I thought he might cut his hand and leave me, but it did not happen at all, the needle sewed me very angrily as if someone had told it not to do so. . . . My other friends laughed at me when the dog laid on me I thought if I could speak, I could send a dog and bite him. I do not like to be a dog's sheet.

The next is by a boy of fifteen who had been turned down as unfit for secondary education. He was good at science, where his unusual capacity for imaging and visualising a process stood him in the same good stead as in his imaginative writing. The following extracts show this quite clearly. He came from a poor home, and was very thin and small for his age, and he was also much younger than the average candidate who takes the secondary entrance examination. He is describing a train journey.

[1] Probably *ekitambala* which can mean scarf or piece of material, etc.

(11) Fortunately I was packed with my friends in the same box. I saw many things in that box because I was near a crack where I could see everything except the side opposite to me. I heard people calling out 'Mombasa'. I was packed in a big coach but I did not notice what it was. At mid-day I heard a thing making a noise. 'Chicle-chile-chile-ch-e-e', and so on. I was at the top now. I saw trees which passed quickly. Now it was the tenth day since I cam from England. It was a long journey. I fell asleep. I dreamt people were pressing me with their feet and it made me dirty. Afterwards I was picked up and was hung on a string crossing the street. I felt angry because I was in the sun. While I was still in my dream I was awakened by a big noise which frightened me, It sounded like a gun, 'Poo-oo', I looked round. I saw blue with a mixture of white, green and brown things. I notice I was being tumbled about. The blue thing was the sky and clouds the green was trees and grass and brown was earth. I found myself in a shop opened by two men. I was amazed, because I had never seen a Black or Brown man before and I was frightened too. Because I was white they took care not to make me dirty,

In the oral discussion preceding this composition the children had suggested that they would begin the life-story as a seed, a thought which had not occurred to the teacher. But cotton means good seed to the local African children for it is a rewarding cash crop. They were, moreover, fully acquainted with the history of cotton through their geography lessons. The significant point here is the variety of expression of the responses to, and interpretation of, the facts.

As time passed and we grew a little more knowledgeable and experienced, it became easier to think of fruitful and stimulating subjects for original writing. In the third and fourth year, 'A page (or a chapter) out of my autobiography', became one of our best subjects. I used the beginning of the life of Booker Washington and two short extracts from Noel Coward's *Present Indicative*, and supplemented these by describing scenes from my own childhood.

We used the 'Bus Journey' theme at a more mature level in the third and fourth year. The model was D. H. Lawrence's description of the gossipy wife left behind on the way to

Mandas, in *Sea and Sardinia*.[1] This struck very near home, and the compositions written under the title, 'An incident on a bus (or train) journey', always brought in a satisfactory harvest.

'Noises at Night', which I had used in England, was easily adaptable for African children at a more advanced stage, and extremely useful for extension of vocabulary. Many African children are very interested in dreams (as are English children), and 'A Dream' or 'A Nightmare' also became a best subject.

'The worst storm I ever experienced' proved very rewarding. For some time I was stuck for a model. I rejected as too complicated the description of the storm at the beginning of *A High Wind in Jamaica*, and storms at sea were no use, of course. Through the helpful suggestion of a lecturer in the English Department at Makerere College, I used Aldous Huxley's description of the storm in 'The Rest Cure'.[2] which I slightly adapted. Everybody was immensely impressed by the model, probably because the vivid description of the violence of the storm aptly expressed what the pupils themselves had often inarticulately felt about local storms, which are violent and dramatic.[3]

I have said that the discovery in the Art lessons of the children's extraordinarily limited knowledge of the fruit and vegetables in the local market gave rise to the composition, 'An African Market', or 'A Visit to the Market'. The preparation for this lesson took no less than three forty-minute periods, and I again used extracts from *Sea and Sardinia*, very slightly adapted, as the model.

The first period was entirely taken up with handling and examining and discussing the fruit and vegetables which I had

[1] D. H. Lawrence, *Sea and Sardinia*, p. 108 (1934).

[2] Aldous Huxley, 'The Rest Cure' from the collection of short stories *Brief Candles* (1948).

[3] Some students in training who were attending this lesson said they thought the passage too difficult. Later, when they heard and saw the result, they confessed they would have been unable to achieve them. This merely shows that they themselves had been the victims of the unimaginative underestimation of their own past teachers.

brought into the classroom, and entering their names and the words we would need to state their qualities and attributes into their language-books. This part of the teaching, I found, was one of the most interesting and instructive exercises for the teacher. When I said, 'Hold the egg-plant or the cucumber to your cheek', they obeyed gingerly. As the outstanding characteristic of these vegetables consequently dawned on the pupils (the classroom was hot), and I elicited that we needed the words 'cool' and 'smooth' (also 'shiny', etc.), broad smiles spread over their faces, and some people tried to hang on to a cucumber or egg-plant to keep it pressed to their cheek for coolness. Others reacted differently, shivered, and passed the thing on quickly. When I produced the expression 'cool as a cucumber', their recent experience rendered it intelligible at once, and it was much appreciated; so was the expression 'green as a cucumber'. There was a great deal of apparent enjoyment from discussion of smells and tastes. 'Scent' and 'fragrance' appealed, and the words, 'succulent' and 'delicious' were very popular. The Baganda often refer to grenadillas as 'apples' and I bought some Australian apples to demonstrate what this foreign fruit really was. Everyone ate a small piece, and quite a number did not like the taste, for it seemed rather tart to them.

This particular composition was one of the best for extension of imagery and vocabulary, and never failed to be rewarding. A careful and systematic study of the evocativeness which certain words, phrases, and turns of phrase evidently had for our African pupils would prove revealing. Sibilant words, for instance, seem to exercise a strong attraction.

There was a basic minimum of vocabulary common to all pupils but no one pupil, of course, retained the whole vocabulary which had been discussed; each individual assimilated according to his taste and capacity, and squirrel-like used this newly acquired little store as required in subsequent situations, both oral and written. Occasionally a term was subsequently misapplied in a different context, as one would expect; but the rarity of this occurrence led us to observe that vocabulary and phrases learnt in connection with the original imaginative writing, combined with those taken over from imaginative reading matter which had caught the children's imagination, formed the language most easily remembered and re-applied.

To conclude this consideration of the children's original imaginative written work I should like to discuss one last subject. When we started, this subject was, as I have stated, definitely outside their scope.

In England I had used an extract from Rupert Brooke's poem 'The Great Lover' to help to stimulate the response required in order to get the children to write a poem or piece of prose on the same theme. I had also, as mentioned earlier, found the subject, 'My favourite dish', both popular and rewarding.

In the circumstances both these subjects appeared quite useless and beyond the imaginative participation of our African pupils. However, we ventured to try out the subject 'My favourite dish' in view of the marked extension of observation and imagery, the development of aesthetic appreciation, and the increased command of simple English. More important, the 'climate of feeling' was completely different from the climate into which we were at first received. The number of dishes the local African, even the more sophisticated African, is familiar with is limited, and to our foreign eye the main ones have not much to recommend them, aesthetically speaking. The preparation, including the vocabulary, was much enjoyed, and contrary to our expectations the children tackled the composition with great zest and wrote at considerable length. But to us the results were most interesting in relation to finding in the children's work a dawning recognition of a new conception of, and way of looking at, humdrum every-day things, such as food.

Given below are two full-length examples from English children and two from African children. The sentimentalist will say, 'Ah yes, but of course children are the same all over the world'. This is a superficial judgment: the work itself is the outcome of an approach based on the opposite conception, that of 'the beautiful variety of things'. The quality of living is enhanced by the riches of variety, and it is the educator's aim to discover and encourage these riches, not to ignore them or attempt to iron them into uniformity.

In the two English examples the spontaneity of the imagery is obvious. In the first example it is zestful and exhilarating, in the second, delicate and sensitive. Both are typical of the writers.

In the two African examples the imagery is being carefully coaxed and nurtured and is reminiscent of the first steps of a child learning to walk; but there is promise. Certain qualities which are distinctive of the African writers (such as directness and economy of expression) are different from the characteristic features of the English children's writing.

(1) *By an English boy, aged twelve years, eight months.*

My Favourite Dinner

Some years ago, I had just been indulging in a strenuous game of foot-ball, when I felt hungrey. This was not unusual but that day I had felt as if the pangs of hunger were gnawing at my vitals. Having bidden my friends 'good-bye' I departed homewards.

When I reached home, my mother noticed my muddy boots and drew my attention to them and also remarked that she had made a special dinner for me. I made a few sarcastic remarks, mainly to the effect that I expected something like partridge.[1]

Mother said:

'Stay in the drawing-room until I call you.' When she called me I was a little dubious at first for I suspected a practical joke. None came however and I followed her into the dining-room.

There, on a spotless-white table-cloth perching jauntily on a blue plate, lay a 'dream' of mushrooms, frid tomatoes, chips and a large chunk of fried steak. I literally dribbled. Then I waded into the spread with gusto. In ten minutes my plate was clean. Then Mother came in with my second course. When I saw it, my eyes stood out of my head, and my mouth went dry. It was past watering.

Amid a swamp of fruit juice and cream, there lay a perfect fruit-salad. There were, strawberries, chopped up apples, pears and

[1] This was just after the war.

bananas, plums, and nearly all the fruits excepting tomatoes and grapefruit.

For the moment I thought I was dreaming but when I tasted it I was very glad that I was awake. I did my best but I couldn't quite finish my very large plateful.

When I had finished my mother asked me if I like it! I assured her that it was the best dinner I had ever tasted, whereupon she said, 'Well, come and help me wash up'.

I grunted.

(2) *By an English girl, aged twelve years.*

My favourite dish

I prefer lemons to anything besides snow-fruits, and toffee-apples. On the outside a lemon is oval in shape, apart from a slight bulge at the end. Its skin is smooth, yellow in colour, and tastes very bitter.

On the inside it has a stringy piece down the centre which is woolly. Round the piece is the eatable part of the lemon. This part is made up of boat-shaped portions which are covered with a fine skin. Inside this skin there are many tiny cells containing juice. Lemon tastes sour and yet not bitter.

They make my mouth feel fresh and smooth, and leave a pleasant taste after I've eaten them.

Both these children attended a large mixed County Grammar school in North London. They were both in their first year.

(3) *By an African girl, aged fourteen years.*

My favourite dish

English[1] potatoes are my favourite food.

One day when I went home I found my mother frying potatoes. I did not know what she fried them with, because as I was walking along the road near the little path which goes home, I smelled a very good smell which was coming from my mother's kitchen. I said to myself, 'What a good smell, I am very lucky, I am very hungry and tired but I am going to eat. I will be quick.' I walked very quickly.

When I got home I found my mother frying some potatoes, and she said to me 'Justine, you are very lucky because I am cooking

[1] Sweet potatoes are the usual potatoes eaten by the local Africans and are a staple food.

your favourite food.' 'What is it, is that English potatoes?' I said. 'Yes,' answered my mother.

I went into the kitchen and looked at what it was, then I saw very good potatoes with shining soup added with onions and tomatoes, also Kimbo.[1] I was very happy and I went into the house to change my dress supposing I might spoil it when I was eating. I hoped that I would eat very much. I was very happy.

As I was changing my dress, my mother was cleaning the table, I heard the spoons and plates rattling. I ran very quickly and asked my mother, 'Is the food ready? I shall be quick.' 'It is ready, Justine,' she answered.

There were my little sister and two brothers, we sat down and started eating. Because I liked it very much I did not wait for the Grace, my sister and brothers started laughing at me. I did not care about them. Before I went to eat my mouth was watering already. The soup of those potatoes was marvellous to look at, I ate as much as I could until I was satisfied, at the end, by mistake I swallowed a whole potatoe without chewing it and it choked me, my mother said, 'Do not eat very quickly even if you are hungry. There is other food here.' I said, 'I am satisfied but I do not know why I have swallowed the big one.' We then finished eating, but I ate a lot, and it was very nice, it got into my stomach very well because it was well cooked. So I have never eaten such food since.

(4) *By an African girl, aged fourteen.*

My favourite food

One day my mother told me to go and see my grandfather because he was very ill. I went to see him with my little sister. Her name is Kisa.

On the way to our grandfather my sister began to cry. 'Why are you crying Kisa?' I said. 'I am very hungry, I can not move from this place,' she said. [that is 'I cannot go a step further!'] I put her on my back and went to see our grandfather.

He was quite better and he was able to eat. After that, we came back home.

When we were nearly at our home, my sister told me to put her down, before I put her down, I smelled a fine smell. Then I put her down and ran home to see what my mother was doing. I found my mother frying meat that meat was very tender.

[1] Kimbo is the local cooking fat.

I sat near her, and started looking as I am doing now, my eyes started out of my head, and my mouth watered. I saw my sister coming along. Kisa said to our mother, 'I am starving mother, help, help.' So my mother gave her a piece of that fine, tender meat. Kisa ran very quickly to eat it. As she ate it greedily it made her choke.

My mother gave me a piece of it, and I said, 'Thank-you,' to her. That piece of meat was so small, I put it in my mouth, I chewed it only once and swallowed it as quickly as I could. The meat went down like a car on the Ntebe road.[1]

My brother said, 'Let us go and play until lunch time.' so I said, 'No, no if you want to play, go and play by yourself.'

My mother told me to be ready for lunch. I was very happy, I began to jump like a bird. I was happy as a cat catching a rat.

I washed my hands, and sat down. My mother gave me a very large piece of meat, and I started eating. The meat I had was swimming in gravy. Since I was born I had never had such a good meal as that.

Both the African pupils were in their second year with us, that is in Junior Secondary II.

In four years we had come a long way since we started to investigate and learn if it were possible to find for African children, through a foreign tongue, a means of rousing in them the slumbering 'power to translate the world into some particular language of their own'.

Children are their own best protagonists. In conclusion therefore, an example is given below of a piece of original writing, inspired by the study of autobiographical literature. It is written by a boy of average intelligence, aged sixteen, in the first term of his fourth year with us.

My most vivid childhood memories

I was born at Mombasa, the eastern coat of Kenya. I do not know the real date of my birth, because my mother did not take the trouble to write down the date of my birth. My father was among the soldiers in the last world war, and he did not know the date of my birth. But I was told that I was born when the war had just begun. Therefore I think that I was born towards the end of 1939.

[1] A road notorious for speeding.

At that time Mombasa was not a very big place and there were not many shops.

I remember that when I was about four years old, I had just one Kanzu. I used to take it off and remain naked, because Mombasa is a hot place. I did not think that it was bad to walk about without a Kanzu, near the ocean. I had many friends. One of them was called Juma.

Juma was older than myself, and he was a very naughty boy. My mother told me not to walk about with him, but when I told him about it, he told me that she wanted me not to have any real knowledge while I was still young. And he told me that we should go to the railway station every time we saw the train, and then beg for money from the passengers when they came out of the train. I remember when I begged for money from an Arab, and he gave me two shillings. I brought the money to my mother, and when she asked me where I had got the shillings, I told her that the money was given to me by an Indian, who bought cocoanuts which I had collected near the shore of the ocean. That was a very good lie. My mother seemed to be very happy about it, and she told me to wash my Kanzu every time it was dirty, so that my customers would not call me a dirty boy.

One Sunday morning, my mother told me to go to church, because there was a visitor who wanted to go with me to church. When we were about to go, I heard the noise made by the train. I escaped from the visitor, and went to the station to beg for some money. I did not know how my mother and the visitor knew that I was at the station. They came to the station, and they found me crying, because I had been beaten by a swahili boy. My mother asked the boys who were near me, and they told her that I was beaten due to my selfishness. 'That boy doesn't want us to get any money. He wants to beg from every passenger that comes out of the train. Last Saturday he got two shillings, and then he had been begging from those Arabs who would give us some money also', the boys said. My mother seemed to be very sorry when she saw me crying, and I thought that she would not take any notice of what they said. She took me home, and she told me not to go there again.

The next day Monday was a very bad day. When I woke up early in the morning, I felt very happy. So I determined to go to the station and buy some rice without telling my mother. I went to the station with Juma, and my mother saw us from a distance. She followed me and she found us eating some cakes, for rice was no ready yet. When I saw her I rushed away and thought up reasons which had taken us there. When she came back, she would not listen to any of my words. She brought the heaviest stick that she could find, and I was beaten to the point of death. She told every person who came to our home all that I had done. Some people used to be kind and said that was done by every boy of my age, but the others said that I was very foolish, and I should be taken to prison for that. From that day I learnt that the world was dangerous because as far as I remember, that was the first time I saw my mother being very cross with me.

It was a terrible grief to me when I heard that my best friend had died. Juma tried to swim in the ocean, but I did not know how he came to forget all his knowledge of swimming and then died. A very few days before his death, he had told me to go to the ocean, and he would teach me how to swim, because he said that he was an expert in swimming. After his death I felt very lonely, and began to stay at home with mummy, because there was not anybody who could be as helpful to me as Juma.

I was forced to go to church every Sunday, and I remember the reason why I was interested in Sunday Services. Shima-la-tewa was the church I used to go to. When I went to church every Sunday, I felt very sad when I saw the boys who were even smaller than myself, wearing very white Kanzus. And these boys had their seats in front of us. They had their clean mats near the place where the Reverend used to sit. I wanted to be among those boys, but I had not joined the school yet, sometimes I told my mother to wash my Kanzu very nicely so that I might go with my other friend who had just started in that school. When I used to go on Sunday, I did not feel very happy, because some boys did not want to talk to me. And others had seen me near the station on their way to school, so they did not think that I was a good boy.

Whenever I saw a boy going to school early in the morning, I felt very sad, and sometimes told mother to send me to school as soon as possible. 'Behave well, stop begging for money and do what I tell you to do. Then I shall send you to school'. Mother said to me whenever I told her about my education.

I tried to behave very well, but I could not help it always. Whenever I heard the train I wanted to go to the station. One day I heard the train, and what I did was to rush away. Before I reached the station I saw my mother. So from that day I abandoned this idea.

One day when I was about seven years old, I saw a man who was very kind. He talked to my mother with a cheerful voice, and I remember when he told me that he wanted to take me to my father who was in Uganda. I felt very happy when I heard that my father wanted me, but I was troubled when I was told that mummy was not to go with me. After a short time with the visitor, I was told that we were going to Uganda the next day.

I did not sleep happily that night, because of leaving my mother. The next day we went down to the station, and my mother was getting more and more troubled. I remember when she said 'Shall I ever see you again?' The train came and when we were about to leave I saw her weeping, and I wept also. Then I began to think that perhaps it was something very important, which was going to happen to me.

I sat near the window, and the train passed through places which I had never seen before. I knew very little Luganda because my mother used to speak swahili to me. The man who took me to my father knew very little swahili. I was very frightened when I saw a white man in our coach, collecting some pieces of paper from the passengers. I think they were called tickets. That was the first time I saw a European. I was familiar with Arabs and Indians, because there were not many Europeans at Mombasa at that time.

At last we arrived in Uganda. The place was very dull compared to Mombasa, and my father seemed to be very very happy. My mother had named me Mabuso according to our customs. But my father changed my name. I remember we had a tea-party, and from that day, I came to be known by the name of James Hannington Ssali.

James H. Ssali, Senior II,
Age 16.

PART II

THE PROBLEM IN OTHER MEDIA

3

POETRY

Luganda is a highly onomatopoeic and alliterative language, for example:

matulutulu	at crack of dawn
olusalosalo	ditch
okugalangataana	to be clumsy
walugufu	very thin person
ppikipiki	motor cycle
cakacaka (c pronounced ch)	noise of water dripping through leaves or thatch.
kucekukacekuka	to be smashed to pieces.

We kept this well in mind when we first introduced poetry into our English lessons. We began with nursery rhymes, lullabies, poetry from the Bible and folk-songs which had a universal application; national folk-songs or ballads (like Robin Hood) need for their true appreciation a knowledge and understanding of the whole background which gave rise to them.

I had always greatly enjoyed teaching poetry to English children, thanks mainly to Norman Callan's book, *Poetry in Practice*,[1] which had been my constant guide, and had never failed me. It had set me off on lines whose infinite promise I had only begun to explore by the time I came to Uganda. We had discussed Norman Callan's approach and methods at teachers' courses, and other teachers had also enthusiastically reported on the results of using his methods. Now I found myself in a

[1] Norman Callan, *Poetry in Practice* (1938).

situation where I should have to readjust all this, for there was no book known to me of the calibre or imagination of Callan's, dealing with the subject of teaching poetry to African children. I was pretty sure the fundamental principles of the approach would remain the same, for Norman Callan had gone into the matter far too deeply not to touch on issues which would ensure some constructive contribution to the problem.

Once we could find a way of tackling it, we were sure that poetry, like painting, would play a considerable part in extending the children's imagery and imaginative participation. If we succeeded it would be a powerful agent in fostering a positive response to literature as the richest form of language expression.

Many European children frequently participate creatively in poetry long before they seriously participate in prose. I heard a two-year-old chanting 'Wantamotocar, wantamotocar'; and on a London bus I heard a three-year-old:

> And the bus
> and the bus
> is going round
> going round
> the co-or-ner. [With repeats]

These two children are potential appreciators of poetry by reason of having created some in no matter how humble a way. This potential appreciation is too frequently silenced by the time the child has had a few years at school.

My colleague and I had no knowledge of a comparable nature with regard to African children to encourage us. We had to start completely in the dark. Nevertheless we tentatively approached our poetry-teaching along the same lines I had found worked in England; that is, from three angles:

(i) Choral-speaking and acting;
(ii) Reading poetry purely for pleasure. Teacher reading to the class, and occasional written exercises arising out of this;
(iii) Writing poetry.

As there is no such thing as an anthology suitable for a class or series of classes, each child had an exercise book into which he wrote, and illustrated himself, the poems we had decided we particularly wanted to keep. My colleagues and I selected the poems and tried them out after much discussion and searchings through our libraries. The pupils helped us to decide which were the ones to put in the permanent collection. The poems were either cyclostyled or copied from the board. This copying was by no means the sterile kind of thing it may sound, for practically none of our pupils had ever *seen* a poem. The first four books of their standardized English course did not include anything so frivolous as poetry. Hence they were totally unaccustomed to its appearance, shape, lines and pattern (verses, etc.) on the printed page. Until they had had a fair amount of experience of it, and had begun to grasp the significance of the format, especially when reading aloud, they could not understand that it mattered very much how you wrote out a poem, even after many exhortations from the teacher.

(i) CHORAL-SPEAKING AND ACTING

The most rapid way of involving a whole class in a poem is to choose one which is suitable for choral-speaking or for choral-speaking combined with acting. (The solo parts can be spoken and acted by individual children, the narrative and refrains, etc., can be parcelled out to different groups according to their voices.) We began with folk songs which were variations of ancient rigmaroles involving a great deal of repetitive pattern, like the Appalachian one, 'I bought me a cat', and 'My father he died and left me twelve cows', and 'Soldier, Soldier, won't you marry me?' and a number of others of the same kind.

These were an unqualified success; the mild passive resistance, born of suspicion of the unfamiliar, changed first into incredulity, then into excited interest, and eventually to full-throated participation. We felt considerably elated. Moreover, at the end of a forty-minute period, the children were able to repeat the whole poem effortlessly, and did so all over the playground.

To begin with, all poems appealed equally to all classes, as the medium was equally new to all, and because the type of folk poetry we were using has an ageless appeal. We had introduced these poems by buttoning them on to the Africans' love of singing, by saying, 'When you sing in your language you use and arrange words rather differently from when you speak ordinarily. We do the same, and sometimes we don't sing them, we speak them. The human voice is still the instrument, but it sounds different'. This explanation always appeared to satisfy, and in any case the class was so soon swept into participation that there was no time for anyone to develop any doubts. Once they *had* participated there was no mistaking the interest and response.

Gradually, we also introduced more serious poems into the older classes. Here we had discussed at length what we had observed in their emotional responses, in as far as we were able to evaluate and interpret these. Their emotions are largely ritualized, and this influence is still very apparent, however much African children are urbanized. We therefore decided that they were likely to be most in sympathy with the monumental (often deceptively uncomplicated) emotions, such as grief over death or great loss. We therefore introduced such ballads as 'Edward' which did in fact produce an immediate response, as did also the 'Lament over Jonathan'. I shall not easily forget the pregnant silence which filled the room when I came to the end of the first reading of 'Edward'. Later on I obtained gramophone records of a number of these songs or ballads, and these were listened to with rapt attention and expression.

One of the real difficulties was rhythm. This we were in no way prepared for, as one of the most frequently quoted beliefs about Africans is the one about their inborn sense of rhythm. What is not realized is that it is a sense of rhythm confined, not unnaturally, to African rhythms, and that European rhythms are wholly strange to the African ear. This is particularly true of poetry, where the rhythm-unit is the syllable, and where the rhythms depend on stress. Such apparent stress as one finds in Luganda is length not strength, and is represented in the new orthography by a double vowel (for example *kaakati*, *bataano*, *onookola*, *okubuula*, etc.). Judging by the delight on the faces of the children, as well as the approval they voiced, European rhythms must strike the African ear as agreeable or entertaining; but our pupils found them almost impossible to imitate, just as they find inflection most difficult in spoken English. This is certainly, to a very great extent, due to characteristics in their own language and way of speaking, apart from the all-important matter of stress. All words in Luganda end in a vowel and many begin with one, in which case the last vowel of the preceding word is dropped. So great is the elision that in the top classes of the Primary school, children will write their own language as if the phrases were one word (*omusananga-gwakanyo* for *omusana nga gwaka nmyo*, *nejaneyitakumpinemporogoma* for *n'ejja n'eyita kumpi n'empologoma*, etc.); few pronounced mouth or lip movements are made, and this is very trying to a European who is not very familiar with the language and who is endeavouring to follow a conversation in Luganda. The pupils naturally carry over these speech habits into English; hence 'butter' is pronounced 'butt', 'water', is 'wat' and 'money' is 'mun'. This persists to the bitter end. Just before School Certificate a boy came into the school certificate class and said 'I want to speak to Apple'. I asked him to repeat what he had said and he did so. Even after four years in the school I did not at first realize that he meant a boy called Apollo.

In the poem 'The Soldier', the children always said 'ohsoljersoljerwonyoumarrme?' with no indication whatsoever of variation of stress. We tried everything we could think of, including clapping and marching, to convey the concept of European stress, that is strong-weak rhythm, not length rhythm. The children entered into everything with zest, but we remained defeated in the end. There was certainly considerable improvement, and the most rewarding kind of practice proved to be the very simple rigmaroles which could be broken down into extremely short passages, even single lines, spoken by different voices. It certainly helped the pupils' spoken English in a most marked way. For one thing, their attention had now been drawn to the matter of strong-weak rhythm, and the most intelligent pupils were interested, and eager to say the words in as 'English' a way as possible. They now made a conscious effort to do so, just as an intelligent and interested English child will make the same effort with spoken French, for example.

One of the most unexpected successes was Alfred Noyes' poem 'The Barrel Organ'. I thought the children would enjoy it as 'sound'. I knew that the European seasons would be beyond their imaginative participation and that the imagery belonged to a peculiarly English context; but I thought I could at least attempt to put over the Englishman's (and the townsman's) joyful participation of the Spring as a contrast to the dark and cold of Winter when all fields are fallow, and only Spring, the time for planting and sowing, can bring promise of fresh supplies of food. This introduction was respectfully listened to, but I need not have worried, as once the poem had been read nobody cared a straw for what it was about; they simply wanted to go on repeating it, which they did, chorally and otherwise. It was impossible to stop them. They learned an extraordinary number of the lines, seemingly without effort. One morning, when I came to school, I was startled to hear from the other side of a bush, a cheerful voice declaiming with considerable abandon, 'Come down to Kew in lilac-time, in lilac-time', etc. (with the correct stress!). It was joined by another voice, just as fervent. It seemed an extraordinary thing to hear issuing from a clump of aloes on the equator, and I shuddered to think of the comments any educationist might, not unjustifiably, have made, had one chanced to drop in that morning. But human beings persist in escaping from theories and African voices ecstatically exclaiming 'It isn't far from London' continued to be heard in the most unlikely places.

We considered that choral-speaking (poetry and poetic prose) was an activity that must on no account be dropped, both from the point of view of the enjoyment it gave and the influence it had on pronunciation and inflection.

(ii) READING POETRY FOR PLEASURE AND (iii) WRITING POETRY

We had introduced poetry at the beginning of the second year, that is, with the classes we had already taught English to for one year, and with the new classes which had been carefully selected. Though poetry can be one of the most potent aids to learning English, it cannot be introduced until a basic minimum of language is known.

The two approaches of reading poetry and writing poetry were interdependent. Just as the appreciation of paintings grew out of painting pictures, so the appreciation of poetry grew out of writing it, though once again models were needed.

> ... poetry is so valuable, because it is by nature the expression of thought in concrete terms, that is, parabolic expression, and so calls for the imaginative effort that is needed to make any teaching or learning alive. *But the only way for children to learn to make this effort is to write poetry as well as to read it.* To get insight into poetry one must learn to use the poet's approach. When this is done, reading becomes appreciative, not merely absorptive. Even though a child's poetry may have no value (that is very unlikely), writing it will make an emotional outlet and will render his reading (that is, his criticism) positive ...
>
> ... Children have many qualities that go to the making of poets, and to give them no opportunity for writing poetry is to waste those qualities ... but good results cannot be got without a tidy way of going to work, ... merely to encourage the writing of poetry, without saying how to do it, is like expecting a child to spell who has not learned his alphabet.[1]

'Children have many qualities that go to the making of poets' ... we thought it was particularly important not to

[1] Norman Callan, *Poetry in Practice*, pp. 22 and 23 (1938).

waste those qualities and potentialities in our African pupils since in their country African poets had yet to emerge.

We began with very short nursery rhymes, having first asked the children what sort of things they said and sang to the babies of the family when they had to look after them, console them, entertain them or hush them to sleep. We hoped by this means to extend already familiar experience. The following examples of children's original work will, to some extent, indicate the degree and quality of their participation. The work was undertaken immediately after the various lessons on nursery rhymes, and many nursery rhymes were read and talked about. Some of the poems were written in spare time, and once writing poetry had started, I not infrequently met someone in the playground holding some scrap of paper which was shyly proffered and on which the child had made some attempt to write poetry. It must be ever kept in mind that the pupils were writing in a second language, not their mother tongue. This was a much more demanding exercise than for an English child to write poetry in French or German, for these are allied languages, whereas the African children were attempting to write a European language, having been brought up in a Bantu one.

Nothing has been corrected in the examples given in this chapter other than an occasional spelling mistake (for example, 'chicken' is almost always confused with 'kitchen') and a little punctuation. The uncorrected originals would have been quoted but are no longer available. When various forms of original writing began to be developed, we invented a 'Book of Merit'. Every pupil who had shown in his writing the seeds of the prose that is art, wrote his corrected work into this book. Before entering the work in the book the corrections were discussed with him, as we did not consider it sound to copy uncorrected work into the Book of Merit. The pupil's name was read out at prayers, and sometimes his work was read out to the school; it was always read out to his class. When poetry-writing started, naturally poems also went into the Book of

Merit. Although the merit was for qualitative things (such as lively imagery) work below a certain standard of technical efficiency was not considered for the Book of Merit. Consequently there were very few corrections to be discussed in connection with this work, and these were concerned with superficial aspects of it, never with any actual alteration of the original. Looking on it in retrospect, we perhaps rather recklessly returned the originals to the writers. It was a very great honour indeed to be allowed to write your work into the Book of Merit and it was a considerable influence in helping to set literary standards.

The following poem was written after a number of nursery rhymes including 'This little pig went to market' had been read,

(1) *By Sengendo (a boy aged 13)*

Poem from Uganda of many years ago about the fingers

The first finger said, 'Let us go and steal everywhere we like'.
The second finger said, 'Where shall we go to steal?'
The third finger said, 'They will catch us'.
The fourth finger said, 'Yes, let us go'.
The fifth finger said, 'I shall not go with you'.

The next poem was written after a number of rhymes including 'Three Blind Mice' and others with 'nonsense' (purely onomatopoeic) refrains, had been read. These caused much enjoyment.

(2) *By Kyeyune (a boy aged 13)*

Hens

Two or five of them are hens,
Some of them are chickens
One of them is bad,
And one of them is good,
Pinity, pinity, pinity,
I want to go to sleep
Oh no, Oh no, chicken,
Don't talk about sleeping
Pinity, pinity, pinity,

Let us go to sleep
Panipal, panipal, panipal,
Who will go to sleep?
Oh dear, Oh dear friend,
We want to go to sleep,
Because of being very tired
Oh dear, Oh dear friend,
See them running away.

The next poem was written after a number of lullabies had been read. The writer's father was a Church of England parson, though he will have conducted his services in Luganda.

(3) *By Wevugira (a boy aged 13)*

Baby

Sleep baby sleep.
Your brother is going to sleep
Your sister is going to cook your food,
    That you may sleep.
Sleep baby sleep
Your mother is going to sleep.
Your father is going to settle your bed
    That you may sleep.
Sleep baby sleep.
Your bed is ready to sleep.
Our God may keep your heart at rest,
    That you may sleep.
Sleep baby sleep.
Your flesh is tired for sleep.
Your moment is ready to start to sleep.
    That you may rest.

We found ourselves in the rare position of having pupils with no preconceived ideas concerning poetry; hence no-one was in the condition, so common among mistaught children at home, of being what I can only describe as 'eggbound' by rhyme. One of the first operations in England was to release the pupils from the impression that the chief criterion of poetry was that it rhymed. The difficulty of keeping up this sort of verbal acrobatics naturally led the pupils to think that writing poetry was beyond the scope of all ordinary mortals who did not possess a special kind of witchcraft. As Norman Callan has pointed out '. . . It is important for them [the pupils] to recognize as many of the patterns of poetry as possible, and not to imagine that rhyme, which, although it is the most obvious, is in some ways the least satisfactory, is the only one.'[1] My first question in any class in England or Southern Rhodesia (where I worked for nearly five years), had always been 'What do you think is one of the chief differences between prose and poetry?' I cannot remember having received any other answer than 'Poetry rhymes'. I may say it was the answer I also got on teachers' courses, and those teachers who did not think of poetry as something holy, were as relieved as the children used to be, to discover that rhyme, intriguing as it could be, was something one did not have to bother about at all unless one wanted to, and then only when one wanted to.

Our African pupils were in no way bothered by any such notions, nor, it appeared, inhibited in any other way with regard to the writing of poetry. The whole class always applied itself with a will. In England I always estimated that if in the early stages one-third of the class produced something (however short) which showed glimmering beginnings, the teacher could consider the effort worth while. With our African pupils the glimmerings were, on the whole, more widely and more thinly spread, but usually two or three of the attempts produced something more than a glimmer.

We gradually went on to longer and more sustained poems. We used the Benedicite for choral-speaking and after a week of psalms (having laid great stress on the fact that these were poems), hymns and prayers of praise and thankfulness, and extracts from the writings or poems of famous men or poets, I suggested that the pupils might like to write a prayer or song of praise. We had discussed in the classroom the kind of thing that gives rise to a spontaneous feeling of thanksgiving or joy—for instance, rains which save the crops, the power of healing in a

[1] Norman Callan, *Poetry in Practice*, p. 30 (1938).

doctor which saves the life of a parent or loved friend; and so on. The following is produced without alteration:

(4) *By Lukyamuzi* (*a boy aged 16*)

A Psalm of Praise

God must be praised,
It is he who made all things.
He is in Heaven always,
Looking at his things
Which he created with his fingers.
All are beautiful to look at.

When I am walking
I ought to thank him
For all that he does.
He gives me wisdom,
He gives me good life,
And also give us food.

When I was about four years old
I thought of God as
The greatest person in the world,
And what I thought was true,
When I was taught by my teacher.
And now I must praise him.

Let him give good understanding
To do all that which is right to do,
To speak in a polite way,
To serve other people
When I meet any difficulty
May I be with him always.

The writer was a boy of intelligence with a discouraging home background; he walked five miles to school and back. He was considered to be an 'awkward' boy, and he occasionally played truant. He was, however, usually responsive wherever anything could be approached imaginatively.

Snakes exercise a powerful influence of fear over all African children. Although the town dweller rarely sees one, snakes are a reality outside the towns, and death from snake-bite is not uncommon. Several times, I read D. H. Lawrence's 'Snake' with the children in the older classes. I always found that this writer's compelling imagery soon overcame the most resistant English children, and this poem at least could be expected to make contact with African children. The idea that anyone could be fascinated by a snake's peculiar beauty to the extent even of hesitating to kill it, struck them rather as a *new* idea than a totally strange one. Judging from their own attempts at writing a poem entitled 'The Snake', half of them, though prepared to entertain this new conception of a snake, rejected it as unpractical (that is, they killed their snakes in their poems). Those who were emerging as the more imaginative in the class (there was a close correlation with their work in painting, though there were exceptions), appeared to have been sufficiently stirred to exploit and linger with evident pleasure over the possibilities afforded by this new vision.

Below are extracts from a number of attempts. One outstanding feature was the way in which so many of the children had absorbed the atmosphere and the strange lilt of the poem. The influence of the poet's imagery is, I think, very evident, and shows just how the right model can in fact stimulate the pupils and rouse their potentialities—those potentialities which Norman Callan reminds us, wastefully wither away and perish if never aroused. We should remember too the practical implications of this wastefulness, for once imaginative potentialities are aroused they can be applied to many fields, not merely to poetry. They are needed in engineering as well as in writing poetry.

It may be as well here to utter a word of warning. Evoking this response and then helping the children to find concrete expression for it, is not easy. It requires knowledge and skill as well as sympathy and much thought. We were fortunate in having had the experience of Norman Callan's approach and methods as a guide. This is not the place in which to give a detailed analysis of the methods used, but it would be unfortunate if I gave the impression that any of these things happened of themselves or, to use a horribly abused word, 'naturally'. It would be equally unfortunate if I gave the impression that the whole thing is the product of a kind of magic or gift on the part of the teacher, so that the idea of training teachers to teach poetry in an imaginative and constructive way is merely an academic question. As in all other spheres of teaching, if it is intended that the teaching should be of the living and not of the dead, then student-teachers must be carefully trained according to their own preferences. No teacher can teach effectively what he himself is bored by, or is out of sympathy with.

(5) *By a boy aged 16*

A Snake

Very cold as coldness can be,
Very long as length can be,
And very fierce its face emerges.
And by its winding the journey enlarges.
From cold, cold; and through a dark hole
the snake usually pushes its body whole.

. . . It moves like a dignified King in his court
But how horrible, how frosty.
How funny how queer.
The snake is always funny, it is queer
And above all it is fierce.

The punctuation of the above is as in the original. Nothing has been altered. Such imagery as 'by its winding the journey enlarges', would have been quite impossible in the first year of English that we had with this class. These pupils had now had two years of consistent encouragement. And of course, as has been said, everybody knew that no one was ever ridiculed or laughed at.

(6) *By a boy aged 17 (in the same class as the previous writer)*

A Snake

It was a rainy season a snake came into my room
It was a blackeyed, stunted creature

Which had been wetted by the chilly weather
And it searched for warmth as it got into the room.

The guest by no means was innocent
It looked eagerly as it raised its tail
Then it trembled and hid itself underneath the chair
And quietly it began to whistle.

This writer disposed of his snake, . . . 'till in the end I stabbed it to death'.

The following poem has been included in its entirety, and has not been corrected. It was written by a shy girl in the same class, whose English, from a technical point of view, was among the worst in the class. How much this was due to her past experiences or to any innate inability, I would not venture to pronounce upon. What is certain, as can be seen from this poem, is that this work gave her an opportunity of showing and expressing potentialities hitherto unsuspected. She wrote other poems, all of the same quality. This one was put into the Book of Merit, and no one was more astonished than she was at this wholly unexpected development which also earned the respect of the class.

(7) *By a girl aged 16*

Poem [Snake]

Slowly, silently the snake comes.
In the lovely shadow tree.
With its silvery colours moves,
Towards the lovely shadow trees.

"Who is that" I said
The silvery coloured snake.
Continuously moving towards the lovely shadow tree
I shouted loudly in the lovely shadow trees.
Angry eyes it looked into the lovely shadow tree
Its tongue moved in its velvety mouth.
easing its silvery body into a hole,
In the lovely shadow trees.

The economy of this poem, apart from its lyrical quality, might well arouse the envy of a more experienced poet.

One of the poems which had been read prior to 'The Snake' had been Walter de la Mare's 'Silver'. This poem was always appreciated by our African pupils, both because of its alliteration, and because of the children's associations with moonlight, which were vivid though unromantic. (Daylight is over by 8 o'clock in Uganda and the brilliant light of a tropical moon has practical implications.) The poem had been read some considerable time ago, but clearly the 'Slowly, silently' of the above is the result of 'Silver'. The children had a great facility for absorbing the alliterative or onomatopoeic phrases from poems, and it is interesting to see how these were then applied with a perfect sense of fitness in a completely new context. This is seen in (7). This is the true, imaginative application of new things properly felt and understood. Another point worth noting is that there was a high frequency occurrence in the children's attempts of some form of the expression 'easing its body'. I do not remember dwelling unduly on this, except in so far as it came into the general discussion of snakes' movements. No child when writing his poem had a copy of D. H. Lawrence's 'Snake' by him. I had collected all the cyclostyled copies which they had been using when I read and discussed the poem. Our own feeling was that it was once more the tactile appeal which had made this impression. They had felt the image in their fingers and hands.

(8) *By a boy aged 15*

A Snake

As I came down the road,
    At one side upon the rocks
There I saw the king of the earthworms
    In a coil on the rocks.
Listening and watching on every side.
    There he was warming himself,
In the warm bright sunshine.
I interrupted him though I did not like,
    He began to move away from my sight.
Very slowly and very smoothly away he went,
    As though the rock was smooth and soft.
But it was the rough and hard rock.

He was more than a man's height in length.
    He was but more than my arm in thickness.
Very black and smooth in colour,
    With a white sparkling belly
As though it was made of glass.

[Etc.]

The format is the boy's own. When I came to the school, this boy could not spell or write one word of English, and I was told by the staff that he could not possibly ever pass any examination. He did in fact pass the Junior Secondary leaving examination and went on to the Senior school. His improvement began to be marked after about one year, although there were many signs before then of his imaginative nature. He had a very delightful sense of humour. He came from a very crowded home where he had no chance whatever of doing any kind of reading or study, and he was very poor. It is obviously a platitude to say that there must be thousands of African school children whose unsuspected potentialities are never roused or discovered; in our limited experience there was more than enough evidence to discredit for ever the glib comment, 'They can't appreciate poetry', or 'Oh, of course they have no imagination'. The lack of imagination lies in the speaker.

I had often noticed in towns the pathetic forlornness of the country African buffeted on the pavement, or gazing hungrily into shop windows. I began to search for poems expressing longing, or yearning for home and familiar things, songs of exile, wish-fulfilment poems and the like. Armed with these I approached my liveliest class of pupils. As I explained that I had brought a new kind of poem they became eager and alert. I explained that these poems dealt with various kinds of home-sickness and wishes. I then plunged straight into 'The Lake Isle of Innisfree', and pointed out the feeling that Yeats must have had exiled in the noise and 'hardness' of the city, away from the soft mists and friendly familiarity of his humble and simple home. (I allowed myself this poetic licence.)

The reception the children gave this poem caused me to see it in a fresh light. It had been ruined for me when I was at school, but now the unpretentiousness of the 'nine bean rows', the bees (Africans are very fond of honey), the mists, and the cruel stone pavements, unsympathetic to the bare, tired feet of the country Africans, gave it a new significance. Nothing seemed more natural to them than the urgency of 'I will arise and go *now*', and the following lines needed no further explanation:

> I hear lake water lapping with low sounds by the shore;
> While I stand on the roadway, or on the pavement grey,
> I hear it in the deep heart's core.

The children knew what that felt like; there were few who had not suffered some kind of exile, from home, mother, parents, 'country' (what we should call a county or district), not forgetting those billeted on strangers or relatives to enable them to go to school.

The following was written after reading some of these poems of exile:

(9) *By a boy aged 15½*

My Day Dream

I will arise and walk in the cold night,
Slowly through forests, all being quiet,
The silvery moon shining so high.
In the cold I will walk and reach the mountains high.

Over the mountains in the moonlight bright,
Over the plains full of morning mist,
The dark clouds moving to the North,
The light cold winds moving to the South.

Here standing on the soil of the lovely Island,
I felt happy when from the sea I felt the bracing wind,
I was free from home-sickness,
And life came to me with great quickness.

The 'sea' is, of course, the lake. No alteration had been made in the poem.

Another point which is brought home to one when teaching African children is that clichés and bathos do not exist for the

African. Partly this is because most of the experiences involved in original written work are first experiences for the African pupil; partly because he is too literal, and partly because of the main point of our problem—his imagery. He translates the new experience into terms of his own clear-imagined daily life. The boy who wrote the following wrote perfectly seriously and in all sincerity:

(10) *By a boy aged 11*

My Day Dream

I will arise and collect my books and go back to school,
In the classroom shall I put my books for my studies,
Great numbers of my friends shall I find there,
    Standing and sitting on the stools,
Buying and eating during break time,
Oh! I will go and have peace there.

To him, coming to school was largely arriving in a promised land, and the feeling expressed in Yeats' poem, as understood by him, he had equated with his own feelings of longing to get back to school. Many of the senior boys have tried to explain to us what it meant to them to return to school. School gave them a sense of security, order and routine, and companionship of friends, all of which produced a feeling of well-being, differing from anything they had experienced outside.

The English child can write in similarly concrete terms. To illustrate this I have given below an attempt written by an African boy of sixteen and some verses written by an English boy of ten in a Primary school in a poor district in London. Both attempts were made after reading and discussing such wish-fulfilment poems as 'If I were Lord of Tartary'. With the English children it was suggested that they should write what they would like if they were Lord of Tartary. The two first lines direct from Walter de la Mare's poem in the second example are remembered, not copied, as no child in this class ever saw the poem. It was an emergency lesson, and the poem was read and discussed only.

(11) *By an African boy aged 16*

My Day Dream

I wish I were a Lord in London, London, London,
I would have lived there happy and peacefully.
The fastest aeroplane, beautiful cars would have been my riches.
I would command everything that I would like best.
A visit to her Majesty's palace, palace, palace.
What would be the sight, sight, sight!
Beautiful chairs, tables with flowers, flowers, flowers.
I would visit the whole world, world, world.
Studying different regions, people and animals,
Then rivers lake, seas, and oceans.
There my life would be decent, like a Lord, Lord, Lord,
Like a Lord living in London!

(12) *By an English boy aged 10*

Tartary

If I were Lord of Tartary
Myself and me alone
I'd have a bedroom for myself
And a gold and silver comb.

If I were Lord of Tartary
I'd eat a leg of mutton
And when at night I go to bed
I'd eat a choclet button.

If I were Lord of Tartary
I'd have a soljers suit
And when soljers came marching by
I'd give them a serloot.

If I were Lord of Tartary
I'd never go to school.
If I did,[1] I'd do some sums
Composition nun at all

There were thirteen verses of this: his English teacher had written on his last report, 'Finds it difficult to express himself'.

Apart from writing poetry there are, of course, many exercises for extending imaginative sympathy, especially in connection with longer poems. After reading and re-reading 'The

[1] The comma has been added!

Ancient Mariner' in the Senior classes (third and fourth year English), I asked the pupils to describe the beginning of the poem as told by the Wedding Guest, and to stop at the point where the Mariner relates how he shot the Albatross. We had first acted this scene. Below is an example from a boy who had had three years' English with us. It is exactly as in the original, including spelling and punctuation.

(13) *By a boy aged 16*

The Story told by the Wedding Guest

Yesterday, when I was going to a wedding with two other guests, a strange incident happened to me. We were walking up the hill to the wedding, when an old and queer-looking man seized my arm. I told him that I was the next of kin to the bridegroom and that he ought to let me go, for the feast was ready. He held me still with his skinny hand, and said in a low voice, 'There was a ship' I became very cross and serious and told him to let me go at once. Then he loosened my arm, but I was spell-bound by the eye of the old man, and so I constrained to hear his story.

He began to tell me the most frightful story I had ever heard. He began by describing to me how gently and smoothly their ship left the harbour. The weather was fine and they sailed along quite well.

Hearing the music, and seeing the bridegroom step into the hall, I tried to interrupt the story, but he continued. Here I could do nothing, but I was terribly spellbound by the story, so I determined to stay and listen. He said that after the ship had sailed for quite a considerable distance, there came a terrible storm which drove the ship toward the South Pole. They came to a land of ice and of frightful noises, where no living thing could be seen. They were terribly cold for ice was everywhere. This coldness went on for a time until a great sea-bird called Albatross, came through the snow and fog, and it was received with great joy and hospitality. It proved to be a bird of blessings and followed the ship as it returned northward through fog and floating ice. It continued to follow them wherever they were going until . . . when the old man arrived at this point, he blushed and his face became pale. I was terribly shocked and I asked him what the matter was. He replied in a low and frightful voice, 'With my cross-bow, I shot the bird.'

After reading Tennyson's 'The Brook', the exercise was 'A chapter (or a page) out of the autobiography of a brook or a river'. The possibilities are endless.

I now come to an aspect of Norman Callan's technique of poetry teaching which, in relation to teaching African children, took on a significance and importance undreamt of by its author. We considered it could be one of the most effective and enjoyable means of helping to overcome the African children's difficulties with stress.

One of the things that he guaranteed would kill poetry in senior schools for all but the hardiest child was the conventional pedestrian emphasis on scansion. Norman Callan completely revolutionized my own approach to poetic rhythm, and made all teaching concerned with it a joy which could be shared with the pupils.

A sharp distinction lies between prosody and scansion, especially in English poetry. The one, from the teaching point of view, is creative; the other purely analytical. A study of scansion begins and ends with the number of feet in a line, and the number of syllables in a foot; it has to assume all sorts of rules which are half the time inapplicable and the other half force rhythm to a beat as monotonous as that of a taxi engine missing on two cylinders. . . . In the study of metre one must have some unit to work from, and although the ultimate unit is the syllable, it is useful to have some rough groupings handy and to give them definite names. These groupings are ready-made in the Classical feet, whose names, furthermore, are usefully descriptive, and widely known. No harm can come of them, that I can see, so long as it is recognized that *they are built on the stress of a syllable, not on its quantity, and that they may be broken up or combined just as the poet wishes* . . . This basic grouping of syllables is the ground work on which can be built up all kinds of metrical variation. . . . All speech has its small pauses and accentuations, quite independent of punctuation: were these not present it would become a gabbled monotone, broken only by commas, full stops, and so on. These pauses and accentuations (stresses) give prose speech its rhythm not different *in kind* from that of poetic speech, but only in degree of regularity. . . . But poetic rhythm has another difference, beside regularity, from that of prose, in that the former is governed by sound and the latter (not entirely, but to a large extent) by intellectual meaning. For this reason the unit of poetic rhythm is the syllable, that of prose rhythm the word. . . . To know that an iambus is 'te-tum' is a useless piece of erudition; but to know that 'the cat', 'expect' and 'attack' are iambuses, in prose or poetry, connects with everyday things.[1]

Norman Callan shows how it is perfectly possible, for specific purposes, to isolate the musical, rhythmic and purely sound aspect of poetry and study it separately before merging it with 'sound and sense poetry' which then is illuminated by the knowledge and understanding gained from the exercises in 'sound patterns'.

In England I had been staggered by the results obtained along these lines, and had had hard work to keep pace with my pupils. In Africa the 'sound pattern' approach naturally touched the very core of all the troubles and difficulties Africans have with inflection in the English language.

I did not, of course, use the names of the classical feet with African children. This did not matter. Having first practised recognition of the number of syllables in English words, it was pointed out that English words have their own rhythm. For example 'gooseberry' (strong-weak-weak) is in waltz-time (dactyl) and 'window' (strong-weak) is in march-time (trochee). We then collected words according to their rhythms, including, of course, weak-strong (iambus) and weak-weak-strong (anapaest). Instead of the names of the classical feet the groups were named after the first word thought of by the children, that is, the 'window' group, the 'depart' group, and so on. This worked perfectly satisfactorily and was maintained by brisk oral practice, for example, 'Give us another word like "yesterday" (that is, strong-weak-weak) but quickly'. This practice caused much amusement and worked wonders in extension of vocabulary. It also produced an effort at getting the right inflection which was totally different in quality from any previous efforts made by the pupils. It was interesting that these words later never seemed to be mis-spelt.

[1] Norman Callan, *Poetry in Practice*, pp. 56-7 (1938).

A book could easily be written on the subsequent developments and promise of future progress. All that can be said here is that our African pupils enjoyed composing sound patterns. The pace was not unnaturally slower than with European children—after all they were working in a second language—but the vistas opened by the approach were in no way less encouraging. Indeed, in an African context, hitherto unsuspected possibilities might come to fruition. All forms of growth, however, need time. It is useless, and educationally catastrophic, to force. Hence we had arrived, at the end of four years, merely on the fringes of infinite promise when our work was unfortunately interrupted and discontinued.

In conclusion I should like to quote examples of early 'sound patterns' by African and English children, which show the same gaiety and delight in, though a different response to, sound in poetry. Finally I should like to give an example from the work of an English child who had the time to develop further from the composing of sound patterns without sense, to the composing of sound patterns integrated with sense patterns.

(14) *By an African boy aged 16*

A Sound-pattern

Yesterday, jingling, galloping
A girl in the house,
Gambolling, singing, laughingly,
Depart on the road.

(15) *By an African boy aged 16*

A Sound-pattern

Reward beneath mankind depart,
Sitting playing football ho
In the house apart the man
Jingling kissing Monday po

Retain a hat a girl support
Learning blackboard rustling lo
From bome reward a con
Underfed singing insult go

Alarm arouse retain depart
Jingling kissing Monday po
On the road within the cap
Sitting playing football ho

A rose suppose a man support
Underfed singing insult go
Overlook the netball cat
Learning blackboard rustling lo.

This was the boy whose poem 'Hens' is quoted earlier. He always took great delight in sound for sound's sake. Perhaps it should be mentioned that the monosyllables invented by the writer, 'ho, po, lo', etc., have none of the associations that they might conjure up in the mind of a European. To this African boy they are sound only. The four-'verse' (that is repeated pattern) sound-pattern is by no means as simple or guileless as it may at first sight appear. Line three of verse one rhymes with line three of verse two, and line three of verse three rhymes (a 'false' rhyme) with line three of verse four. We have assonance—horizontal rhyme—in 'a rose suppose' and the element of balanced repetition, as well as the staccato effect of the extra strong stress in the single nonsense syllables.

(16) *By a girl aged 13, at Kingsbury County School, London*

A Sound-pattern

Now upon the door mat
Sitting in the lane
Fabric eating elder
What a sweet refrain.

(17) *By a boy aged 13, Kingsbury County School, London*

A Sound-pattern with Rhyme

Blowing north wind glowing brightly,
Spotted adders in the sun,
Ancient horses very sprightly,
Killing fishes one by one.

(18) *By a girl aged 14, Kingsbury County School, London*

Requiem for an Airman

Bury me under the wide open sky
Bury me where I can hear the wind sigh,
At the dead of night, and hear the trees cry
With the wind. There will I lie.
Let me hear the drone of the planes
As they plough through the winter rains,
And for my epitaph write:-
Here lies one who took his flight
And now rests his wings at dead of night.

The original of this lies before me as I write.

Frustration is born of unrealized and dammed-up potentialities: psychologists confirm the words of a contemporary poet, 'In the childhood of Judas, Christ was betrayed'.

Are those of us in charge of the childhood of Africa, entirely blameless?

4

DRAMA

Amongst the many things I shirked in the first year was drama. I felt we could only tackle one thing at a time and I was very unsure about what could be dramatic in a second language. I had been involved in various kinds of dramatic work for many years and I had strong feelings about the sore subject of drama in schools. The syrupy tones of 'the children have done it all themselves' roused my least noble instincts; the never-ending performances of School Certificate texts roused passions in me which rivalled those portrayed on the stage, the worst offenders being 'Scenes from *A Midsummer Night's Dream*' and *A School for Scandal.* I found equally repellent the classroom drama of the 'What-ho' variety, where rulers were used as swords. In England we had evolved a number of methods to avoid these clichés, but in Africa I did not know where to start.

Towards the end of the first year I began to give thought to this question. Acting solo parts had, of course, come into the choral verse-speaking, and we acted very short incidents from stories or poems, not for the sake of the drama, however, but to help the children visualize the thing. Repeatedly we had instances of their peculiar difficulty or inability to visualize a sequence of small incidents or actions, and then I certainly turned to the *doing* of it. For example, in the School Certificate English Language paper there is often a question on sentence construction involving the comprehension of sequence and the subsequent joining of short simple sentences to make longer complex ones, usually without using co-ordinate conjunctions. On one occasion the example we were doing was as follows:

He had packed the children's things in the trunk. He could not close the lid. His youngest daughter sat on the lid. He struggled with the lock. He heard his wife calling him from the next room.

(After he had packed the children's things in the trunk, he could not close the lid until his youngest daughter sat on it, when, still struggling with the lock, he heard his wife calling him from the next room.)

There was great confusion. The class was mercifully honest enough to tell me that they could not possibly visualize the sequence (this was after I had attempted to explain it in words). I was forced to fetch a tin trunk from the house, stuff it so that the lid would not close easily, get one of the smaller boys to sit on it, grapple with the lock, post a boy outside the class-room (there were no girls in the form) and get him to call me. The long-drawn-out 'O-o-o-h!' which greeted the end of this performance expressed appreciative illumination. These small incidents did not involve much dialogue, and, as might be expected, the dialogue was the weakest aspect of it. So what would happen if one had much longer scenes depending on much more English speech? I did not feel at all optimistic.

I was at the same time being much bothered by the question of craft, which I had intended introducing at the earliest opportunity. It was becoming increasingly apparent that this was a subject needed by African children no less than by European children. It was equally obvious that it was the creative crafts that were needed, not the deadening, soul-destroying influence of what so frequently in schools passes for 'book-craft'. For one thing, it was clear that the generalization 'Africans have a natural flair for craftsmanship' (because someone had perhaps seen the Benin heads) was another popular fallacy, very wide of the mark. There were no strong traditions of local crafts in our area, and we had no qualified imaginative craft-teacher available at the time. I had pursued a little craft in an amateurish way and my colleague had had no experience at all.

Nevertheless, unskilled as we were, we somehow had to learn to help ourselves. The thing I knew most about was glove puppets, and my colleague volunteered to share the extra burden that introducing this activity would entail. This answered both needs—the need for drama and the need for craft—in a simple and modest way. I was all for small and modest beginnings, for then if failure threatens one can always beat a hasty retreat without the ignominy attending the disasters which can fall upon more grandiose projects. As someone once pertinently pointed out, we learn by our successes, not by our failures. A really crashing failure usually teaches us one thing—to abstain from repetition.

We therefore sat down and made a glove puppet each. We consoled ourselves by telling each other that at least the children could not be put off by the professional standard of our puppets. No one had seen a puppet before, so it was useless to introduce 'making puppets' until (*a*) the children knew what they were making, and (*b*) what they were making it for. I should like to emphasize yet again, the immense importance in teaching, of taking the pupils into one's confidence and keeping them fully informed of what the teacher is proposing to teach them and why. Every child, indeed every human being of whatever age, likes to tackle his work with a sense of purpose. Take the sense of purpose away and what is left? Naturally I include such purposes as 'to make you able to see other people's point of view' as much as 'to help you pass the exam'. I have never been able to bring myself to exclude the latter from my selection of justifiable purposes, since the exclusion seems to me to be both unrealistic and unfair to the pupils.

We each took our puppet to the next English lesson. We had no fixed plans further ahead. We had to be guided by whatever response, or lack of response, we met with in the classroom.

The occasion on which the children first saw a puppet will remain one of my most vivid teaching memories. When I produced it out of a bag every pupil 'froze' after the manner of children playing statues. I inserted my hand and proceeded to work the puppet. The effect was instantaneous and quite beyond anything I had envisaged. I realized I must hand over at once. I asked who would like to take the puppet and gave it to the first and nearest hand that had shot up. As luck would have it, it was the hand of one of the most imaginative boys in the class and one we suspected of having a considerable sense of humour, though we could only guess. (You cannot be witty in a tongue not your own unless you are particularly blessed in more ways than one, and we did not know Luganda. Our conclusion was the result of observation only.) As soon as he took charge of the puppet it became imbued with a form of life I had not been able to give it, but the boy hesitated. I said, 'You must let him speak—in Luganda of course'. After that I became the pupil. Here was a born puppeteer, and here also was a 'born' audience. They knew nothing of the long and distinguished history of the puppet theatre, but its traditions might have been their own, for they did not have to be told. The puppet was now launched on his patter, the audience replied, heckled, and laughed—laughed till they laid their heads on their desks and in the words of Anatole France *ils perdirent le sentiment.* I can think of no other phrase so apt to describe their abandon. When I finally escaped from the classroom, having dragged the puppet away, I was joined by my colleague who emerged from the opposite classroom, hot and dishevelled and still wiping the tears from her eyes. There was nothing to be said. Puppets were 'on', and humour, the cooling fountain we had so often longed for, had at last emerged sparkling from a deep and proper source.

When comparing notes with my colleague I found that she too had intuitively told the pupil holding the puppet to speak in his mother tongue. We had not previously discussed this point, but we had both felt that the spontaneity on which the whole art of puppetry depends would be fettered by the strain and artificiality of a second language.

Just after the lesson I had to rush into the town to buy something and with the two puppets slung over my arm I got into my car. Two workmen suddenly materialized by the side of the car, and, pointing gingerly at the puppets, one of them said '*Bafudde?*' (literally 'Are they dead?') but having the flavour of the English 'Are they alive?'). The experience was repeated half an hour later in the town where some workmen engaged on a building slid down the scaffolding and crowded round the driver's seat to examine the 'little men'.

We went into puppet production, and, as at that time we had no carpentry in the school, I had a simple puppet theatre made privately at the Technical School, to the measurements and instructions given in Lanchester's book.[1] Meanwhile we used a clothes-horse I had had made (they are unknown in Uganda, because they belong specifically to a country where the drying of clothes goes on indoors), or else just a table or desk.

We started a puppet club which functioned on the weekly club afternoon which we had instituted and it ran consistently without a break and with a long waiting list, for four years.

The first puppets made showed the children's lack of skill and were extremely crude, but they had the one essential ingredient, life. Only one or two girls joined the club, but there was a special club for girls under the auspices of an African member of the Y.W.C.A. so that most of them were absorbed by that. (There were only twenty-two girls in the school which numbered over two hundred pupils.) The boys sewed their garments easily and uninhibitedly. African boys sewed even more easily than boys in England because sewing is a profession for them—not merely tailoring, but all kinds of special sewing in shops. Some of the African boys sewed really beautifully.

There was a problem of standards—a problem which hardly occurred in England. African children did not realize when they fell short of certain standards of achievement generally accepted by European teachers; nor had they any idea when they exceeded them, for they had no comparative yardstick either way. One of the first things we had to do was to make enough fuss and give due praise where it was deserved so that children could begin to get the mental and emotional satisfaction from conscious and legitimate pride in work well done. A child in England who paints an outstanding picture, creates a puppet with some special merit, or makes a clay model with some

[1] Lanchester, *Hand Puppets & String Puppets.*

particularly arresting quality, knows it, and benefits from the ensuing self-respect. He knows it from his fellow-pupils' reactions, and mental comparison with things seen elsewhere, as well as from his teacher. In Uganda the children at first only had the teacher's word of praise or blame to go by, and then only the word of the teacher who was doing the teaching. We had no other members of staff who could judge what was being done, and though this certainly also happens in England it is not usually so important in view of the other influences at work. If we praised a piece of practical work the pupil would sometimes ask 'How do you know it's good?'. Gradually, but very, very gradually, in the light of what they had learned and observed and in the light of their growing experience generally, pupils would venture to make a remark about a fellow-pupil's work. By the end of four years, these were being made and accepted freely in the most experienced classes, often happily accompanied by peals of laughter. Once public performances became regular occurrences to mixed audiences of Europeans and Africans, and outside appreciation was added to internal criticism and evaluation, things moved more quickly, and there was a visible increase in the degree of consciousness with which all activities to do with the puppet theatre were undertaken. Pupils began to try things out on their own, and to rehearse in their spare time. Not many did this; it requires a rare degree of critical judgment to understand the necessity for it. The standard of the puppets produced had meanwhile risen each year. The introduction of rod puppets and, finally, in the fourth year, of string and shadow puppets, greatly aided the children's proper estimation of the range of dramatic possibilities that could be fulfilled with puppets.

For the first performance my colleague and I were forced to invent and mostly make the properties and scenery, such as it was. As we sat up at night doing it we reminded each other to what an educational pass we had been brought, and what scorn we should incur in the eyes of many whose opinions we respected at home. But a public performance requires properties and these have to be imagined and invented. No African pupil had ever had direct or even allied experience of such a thing, so it was useless to expect him to imagine and invent as though he had. Whether he ever would, we could not tell, but until we had let him have the experience, and see examples of what could be done, future developments were unpredictable. We made as many of the properties as we could in club time so that the children could see what use was made of scrap material and could, at least, do simple things connected with the properties, such as painting and glueing, etc.

It is quite impossible to give any adequate idea of the difference between those early beginnings, with the children standing on the threshold of an experience so far completely unexplored, and the much later stages, when it was possible to put one of the older boys in almost complete charge of a public performance with the utmost confidence. It was only with certain properties and scenery that they still very naturally required our assistance.

We kept a large tea-chest full of scraps and junk at one end of the Art room and the day on which a little round-faced boy swooped on the cardboard container which had housed a packet of toilet paper and neatly turned it into a canopy for a throne, was for us a day of educational triumph. Moreover, this is an example of pure creative imagination at work. The mind that at once seizes on the potentialities in material and shape and then proceeds to realize them has performed an act of purely creative imagination. That throne was symbolic, for we never seemed to look back after that.

The key to successful puppetry is to put the puppets into action as soon as they are made. When some of their possibilities have been realized, puppets can be made to fit characters already thought of. Complete spontaneity is essential. Set plays and the learning or reading of lines are all very well for the professional puppeteer (and not always so very well for him), but for educational purposes they defeat the aim for which the activity is pursued, namely for the exercise of the imagination.

The amateur puppeteer has one great advantage over the professional: the latter is too often almost wholly concerned with virtuosity. I have seen professional performances given by companies with an international reputation, where this breath-taking technique ended in monotony, as there was no variation of mood, or feeling, or atmosphere, and no attempt was made to move the audience, except to admiration of technique. Puppets have a tremendous range of expression, far removed from the slapstick farce of Punch and Judy. Above all, in their Lilliputian world, they are always near to pathos and in this their appeal is to the Petroushka in us all. Here the amateur puppeteer comes into his own, for he is not concerned with the box office.

When we first started using puppets in England, it was necessary to insist on some theme or story being followed, the children adapting and extemporizing as they liked. Without a theme all that happened was an endless succession of strip-cartoons, strictly non-verbal and usually merely to the monotonous accompaniment of 'Bang-bang, bang-bang, fz-fz-fz-zzzz', etc. Here in Uganda we had nothing of that kind to contend with; in fact I have never at any time met children more at home in the medium than the African children of Uganda.

At the beginning I suggested to them that it was the daily occurrences in the life of human beings that were most suitable for puppetry, and that it was as well to start with something short and simple—a gossipy wife who lets her husband's dinner burn, for example, or a migrant African stopping to warm himself at the fire of a nightwatchman. That was all that was required. The gossipy wife was put into action but with unlooked for variation on the theme. The dialogue was in Luganda, of course, but puppetry has a way of making any language a vehicle of universal communication. The children then got hold of a drum, and without ever having used puppets before produced a beer-feast which caused every prowling child in the vicinity of the art room to come in and watch. (I got an interpreter for this and other rather racy scenes, but at no time was anything ever said which could have offended even the most delicate susceptibilities—the translator was very reliable. I have always been touched by the children's sense of fitness or seemliness.) Puppetry now had the effect that painting used to have in England, children from other classes dropped in to watch, so did odd workmen passing by, so did everybody, except the staff and a certain number of senior, less intelligent boys. As might be expected it was the humourless people who considered themselves rather superior to their fellows, who entertained the notion that we had introduced something childish and silly which no serious student would think of considering. The most intelligent and vital pupils, or shy imaginative ones, were to be found well to the fore of the Puppet Club whatever age they were. Later, when the Puppet Club gained a certain amount of mild renown, but, above all, when there was no mistaking the enthusiasm of the audiences at public performances, then some of the superior ones condescended to climb down from their exalted perches. Exactly the same phenomenon can be observed in schools in England.

The club grew to such an extent that we were forced, regretfully, to limit the numbers. Even then it was really too large for two people to manage. We divided the members into two groups, beginners and advanced, so that the more advanced group could go on raising the standard.

Among the themes chosen by the children themselves were the simple themes from the Bible, such as the Good Samaritan, and scenes from daily life which included one of a quarrel between neighbours about a hen which ate up one of the neighbour's seed-plants. One neighbour was female and had been especially created for the purpose. She was of such an excessively rakish appearance and her manipulator had a way of getting her to stroke her favourite hen in a manner of such unbelievable engagingness, that we never tired of demanding a further performance. It lengthened at every repetition, as they all tended to do, and there was no mistaking the vast potential of wit we now had access to. But above all, the children had a heaven-sent power of self-identification with the puppets which meant they were able, in a matter of seconds to bring about a complete change of mood, taking their audiences, blessed with the same powers of self-identification, with them.

On one occasion the younger group produced a Bantu legend, which we immediately earmarked for public performance. It was this legend which incorporated the Jeyes' throne already mentioned. Bantu legends which are suitable for school use, let alone for puppetry, are extremely rare, and we had to turn to the literature of other parts of the world for our themes. A point which needs to be emphasized in connection with this, is that when these themes were taken over by the children and reappeared in Luganda acted by African puppets, they became something new. They were not just European stories acted by Africans, and it was not just the language that had changed. The Grimm's fairy tale of the fisherman and his wife was most emphatically no longer a German fairy tale: it was something which had not existed before, and judging by the audience's reactions, old and young alike, it was something wholly African. We certainly gazed at it with eyes seeing it for the first time.

The same thing happened when we handed over the second Wakefield Nativity Play to the children, having first explained and discussed it, and read portions of it aloud to the children. At the end of half an hour what they produced had to be seen to be believed—the bare bones of a new play. The same incidents, yes, but translated completely into African terms. It was difficult to imagine that the shepherds had not been conceived of in the first instance as African herdsmen. I shall never forget the reverence of those bringing gifts at the end of the play; nor how moving were the words of the little African peasant puppet who brought a bunch of bananas, humbly excusing himself that it was no bigger, and saying that he knew Jesus was very small now, but the bananas would soon make him grow big and strong. I remember, even now, the face of an old African who was sitting next to me nodding smiling approval of these words.

People often conclude that the person who made the puppet also works it and speaks for it. This is not at all the case. Often someone would make a character puppet and then find that his voice or control of the puppet was not very effectual. Immediately hands would be stretched out from people who wished to try. The puppet would travel from hand to hand till suddenly it would materialize into a character, and on that hand it would stay. It was as if the puppet knew the hand of its 'master'. The maker of the puppet invariably recognized this too, and there was never the slightest hesitation in handing over the puppet to the manipulator. The manipulator was usually the speaker, though not always, and this too was mostly sorted out amongst the children themselves. Sometimes I would congratulate a puppet on his vocal performance and somebody else would pop out and say 'It was me'. In fact so corporate was the effort that I sometimes had no idea of how many people were involved. If anyone was ill or absent, it made little difference; there were at least half a dozen competent puppeteers or voices ready to take over only lending the puppet the flavour of their own interpretation.

Our public performances were always partly in Luganda and partly in English. For the English items or item we usually used poems or negro spirituals where the solo parts could be acted by the puppets and the narrative spoken as choral verse-speaking or sung by a special choir. It is quite impossible to run a puppet club without music, which is an essential feature of puppetry. Through the kindness of voluntary helpers who came to help with the music, we were able at the end of the second year to put on a Nativity play which we had based mainly on Saint Matthew and a number of carols from all countries, finishing with one in Luganda which a boy in the school had composed.

A great deal could be written about puppetry as an art particularly suited to the special gifts of many African schoolchildren. It would seem perfectly possible to train a team of African puppeteers who could produce a puppet theatre which would have a special contribution to make to the puppet theatre on an international level. Whatever type of puppet we introduced the children handled in a way that was fresh and original in our eyes. Both they and the audience had perfect 'puppet manners'. During a public performance, if a puppet dropped something, a member of the audience would get up and return it to the puppet who would thank him; a little conversation often followed with other members of the audience joining in. This sort of banter is by no means an inseparable part of a public puppet performance at home, though this drawing in of the audience is what every puppeteer longs to achieve. There were times when we found it difficult to believe that the Africans of Uganda had not had a puppet theatre for centuries, though I believe many years ago there used to be a Court Puppet at the Court of the King. We were also never without the perfect compère to introduce the programme, draw the curtains, and shift the scenery—in short, be the life and soul of the party. When our first compère left us to become a bus conductor we were sure we would never recover from the loss. We were quite wrong; the next one who took over, in some mysterious way self-appointed, in no way fell short of his predecessor.

Here was a case where the children had no idea of their outstanding gifts. At the end of four years we would have given anything in the world to have been able to take a picked group to give performances to schools in England. These things can do more to bring about understanding and friendship than all the high level conferences in the world.

Puppetry flourished but when the third year came along I decided it was time to take the plunge and try a dramatic performance in flesh and blood.

In considering what to do we felt that the first thing was to be guided by what I can only describe as a feeling of 'fitness' or 'seemliness'. Africans have a very definite dignity of their own. They move well in long clothes, and these enhance the gestures that come easily to them. These gestures tend to be vertical and biblical in character and remind one of the paintings of El Greco. I realize how many hackles will rise when I say that the spectacular unindigenousness of African capers in purple tights or lace cravats is in some way offensive. It offends against the feeling of fitness; it is unseemly. What offends most and is most unseemly is that it makes an African look like a fool and an ungainly fool, which he does not look by nature. I do not feel we have the right to perpetrate this unseemliness. It would work the other way round too. I do not think that a batch of English school-children taught by efficient African instructors to perform the dances accompanying initiation ceremonies for example, would present any less embarrassing a spectacle. *The School for Scandal* indifferently done in an English Grammar School is a bore, but done by African school-children it attains something scandalous never intended by the playwright. If it is argued that whatever is done will be non-indigenous, I would readily agree, but there is a very wide choice from all the dramatic literature in the world. There is no law dictating that a dramatic performance given by Africans must either be drawn from English dramatic literature or, that if an English classic is chosen, probably because it is set for School Certificate, it should be presented to the public.

There is another thing to be considered also. The audiences will be partly, if not largely, African, and to many an African eye some English period costumes are rather shocking. This is not a question of stuffiness, but again of seemliness and custom, and as there is no compulsion to produce English period plays for public performances, it would seem perhaps wiser and more sensitive to confine such performances to occasions where they cannot outrage anybody's feelings or sensibilities.

When I took the School Certificate class to see a European performance of *Twelfth Night* several boys were very shocked, and one boy wrote indignantly that he could not understand that Europeans were not ashamed to put on such clothes and show themselves in public like that. I spent the next few lessons talking myself hoarse in a futile attempt to describe what a theatre was, and what a professional actor was and did, but this was also beyond the class's imaginative participation. They could, of course, pretend to understand, but they could not, in fact, understand. They had never seen a theatre, and they had never come across the profession of an actor. A boy in the pre-School Certificate year who had been to see a film in which someone died, asked nervously whether the actor, on such an occasion, *really* died. He was a very intelligent and imaginative boy, considerably urbanized, who had—not too fortunately—visited the cinema quite often. The question once more illustrates the literalness of the questioner's approach. He discussed the matter at length, saying that they looked so very dead, and the other people looked really unhappy. How could they do all this, if it were not real? It is true that a candidate for School Certificate cannot, in a sense, have his cake and eat it. He cannot entirely keep both his worlds, but there is such a thing as a gentle transition, and we should aid this as much as possible. It would seem wise to make use of our observation of African reactions rather than stupidly to ignore, or even to ridicule them.

In choosing acting material the soundest thing is always to take something extremely simple which is absolutely within the grasp and control of the actors, and then to demand the highest possible standard. I used the book of Tobit from the Apocrypha for a kind of mime-drama in a Secondary Modern school in England. It was eminently suitable for African adaptation. I was anxious to keep the spoken word down to a minimum as I knew that that was where the greatest difficulty would lie. None of the cast had had any experience except for the Puppet Theatre, and this certainly did help. I used the text straight from the Apocrypha and decided to have someone to read the narration. This device worked very well in England in Secondary Modern schools, where the same difficulty arose over speech with the added difficulty of memorizing. It allowed for the maximum of mime and movement but reduced the burden of speech, which, if badly done, could completely wreck the feeling. The language of the Apocrypha was easy for the children to speak, and the clothes were ideal as they were merely draped tablecloths, curtains and pieces of material, with colours that lent richness to simplicity. The girls presented the worst problem. The custom that girls should speak very softly and look down demurely and not at the speaker, is a devastating influence on the stage. I cut line after line, and bundled them off as quickly as possible.

So far, so good. Everybody liked the story, for the theme of the old man sending his son in the charge of 'an hired man' on a long journey to collect an ancient debt, and the marriage of the young man to a woman of his own tribe, etc., might just as well have been African, it was so familiar. But all the time we were rehearsing I longed to know what it would be like if they were speaking in their own language. Finally I asked an African member of the staff if he would kindly translate the thing into Luganda, which he did. I then handed out the Luganda scripts to the cast and suggested that, as the performance was a short one (about thirty-five minutes), we might repeat it in Luganda, especially for those members of the audience who might appreciate it more that way. Everybody agreed to this, and was most co-operative, and we started rehearsing in Luganda. Meanwhile the leader of the Puppet Club, who was an angel in the play, came to me and said, 'Can we alter the Luganda, because we don't speak like that?' I told him he could do anything he liked that seemed to him to make the characters live. How much actual extemporization went on I am not sure, not much I think, as the performance did not vary, but from then on the Luganda performance was incomparably the better one. There was a spontaneity of gesture, an ease and relaxation about the Luganda performance which the European one never achieved. Both had something to offer, but the Luganda one was my favourite and was the more moving. It was *their* performance. I do not wish to imply that there was anything haphazard about it, for that would have made it a bad performance. There can be no art without technique, just as no art can consist merely of technique, and the children carried the technique learnt in the English version into the Luganda one, but in the Luganda performance they felt at home, and this lent their characters a wonderful authenticity. The angel had captured perfectly the subtle combination of seriousness and whimsical humour expressed in the Apocrypha. This quality was also exploited by James Bridie in his modern sophisticated version.

One rather charming incident seems worth recording. I had given the old blind father a proper make-up with a beard, as old Africans also sometimes have beards. The angel later told me with considerable glee that an African farmer in the audience had said, 'Where *did* they get that old man from? Surely they don't take pupils of that age into the school?'

At the end of it all we were more convinced than ever that performances in the vernacular should be encouraged, and we felt that this would have won the approval of Shakespeare himself, for after all it was but an expression of his own philosophy:

> To thine own self be true,
> And it must follow as the night the day
> Thou canst not then be false to any man.

In Uganda these overworked lines acquired a new significance. In the fourth year I introduced a play to be read aloud to one of the middle forms, and I chose Sierra's *Cradle Song.* I shortened it a little by cutting some of the sections which are more difficult to read than to act. I did this as I hoped we might produce an adapted version of it. Again the theme of the abandoned baby left to be brought up in the charitable convent by nuns was a wholly understandable one to African children.

It also confirmed my feeling that the Baganda would have a certain affinity (as long as this line was not pursued too far) for the Spanish, possibly also the Russian, and for very different reasons, the classical Greek. The ritual formality of Spanish good manners, the insistence on courtesy, the fatalism and love of postponement, found ready appreciators among the Africans. I did not have the time to try out the Russian and classical Greek, but it would be an interesting thing to do. Perhaps it would not prove successful, but it would be worth trying.

What does seem to me to be important for a country as young as Uganda, is that its young people should be introduced to world literature rather than to English literature alone. If the psychology of other European peoples approximates more closely to that of the Baganda and is likely to evoke a sympathetic response, then it would seem a pity to neglect such a promising source of material on the somewhat pedantic grounds put forward by some, that translations always fall short of the original.

We had arrived at this point when circumstances prevented us from continuing.

5

PAINTING

Our aim in this field, too, was education in and through painting, not instruction in any set technique. This did not mean that points of technique were excluded here, any more than education in and through language excludes linguistic points of technique. What did this aim 'Education in and through Painting' mean?

In England I had felt reasonably sure about what this aim signified, and had often discussed it with fellow-teachers. As applied in England it seemed to have three aspects.

(1) First of all the child, in being his own artist, that is, in painting pictures of his own, is learning to appreciate the artist's function and difficulties, and at the same time is beginning to become acquainted with a non-materialistic sense of values.

Putting himself in the place of the painter, he is learning that painting is yet another form of expression and communication and that the artist who is a painter, like the artist who is a writer, is first and foremost an interpreter. He interprets what he thinks and feels about his experiences, especially about his visual experiences, in terms of paint; he puts it down in a picture. He can of course translate any experience, or any reflection on experience, into painting; but a good deal of most children's paintings is in fact concerned with what they *see*, and as a teacher I had built upon this fact. It seems necessary to stress at this point that painting is essentially a visual art; this fact often tends to be overlooked or relegated to the background by a number of current theories and 'fashions', such as those that encourage pupils of all ages, including adults, to paint their 'subconscious'. This is not to deny the therapeutic value of various kinds of painting practised largely on account of their clinical merits. It must be remembered that in ordinary circumstances a normal art class is not a clinic, though any sensitive teacher will treat his children and their needs individually.

A child, then, learns that the value of his interpretation will be expressed and recognizable in certain qualities as well as in certain points of technique.

The most important quality, as in written composition, is the integrity with which he has treated his subject. If he has remained true to his own individual physical vision, his own individual manner of interpreting what he sees and what he thinks and, most especially, *what he feels about he sees*, this will be recognizable in his painting. (It is what, in the professional artist, we call his vision and style.)

His own choice, distribution and treatment of colours and shapes will emphasize his personal peculiarity of expression as well as show what he has learnt about a painter's technical difficulties.

A child evolves his own personal vision and style gradually, as a painter does. After four or five years, it should be possible to look at the pupils' paintings and say, 'That was painted by John Parker, that by Betty Andrews, and that by Billy Davidson'. If this is not so, the teacher should examine his approach and methods, for he has clearly failed to establish the individuality and uniqueness of each of his pupils. Naturally some paintings stand out more than others—that is precisely the measure of an artist's unusualness; and they will stand out for a great variety of reasons, some for humour, some for colour, some for vitality, some for a combination of all three. The permutations and combinations are as infinitely rich in variety as man himself. Where the teaching has aimed at preserving this variety it will be evident, for example, in the pronouncedly individual way in which the pupils have all dealt with the same subject, as opposed to the spurious results of the misconceived approach, 'Oh, I let them paint what they like'.

As this was a point I was often asked to clarify further when taking teachers' courses in England it might not be irrelevant to do so here. What has to be understood is that if six painters are true to themselves and their own interpretation when they paint a vase of sunflowers, for instance, then when they have finished there will be six new ways of looking at sunflowers. If, on the other hand, six botanists draw or paint this same subject their aim will be to make an accurate record, not a personal interpretation of it, and if they are good scientists their observations will lead them to record the same facts. A painter who may be interested only in the mistiness of a rose, for example, can, if he wishes, suppress the thorns in order to emphasize the softness of his subject. The scientist cannot, as the thorns are essential to the factual truth of his record. The painter is concerned with a different kind of truth. This does not, of course, imply that a scientist does not often have pronounced personal characteristics in his approach.

(2) This leads to the second aspect of our aim of education in and through painting. Because they themselves paint, pupils are learning to understand their heritage of painting; they will be able to go into a gallery with knowledge to enable them to enjoy and select.

The enjoyment and critical appreciation of paintings in Art Galleries raises once again the question of 'I like what I know'. 'I don't know anything about art but I know what I like' means, in fact, 'I don't know anything about art, but I like what I know'–that is, what is familiar to me, expressed in a style familiar to me.

In England I had been determined that no pupil of mine should make a fool of himself by pointing an ignorant and consequently often a contemptuous finger at one of the world's great masterpieces. Questionnaires were carefully prepared before our visits to galleries, and were followed up afterwards. This method provided some heartening material. I will quote two instances, both from the bottom class in a Secondary Modern School in a poor district of South-East London. The visit had been to the Tate and the children saw only the Impressionists and Post-Impressionists. One of the questions had been, 'How do you think the cat looks on Madame Manet's lap in the portrait the painter painted of his wife?' When I checked over the replies in the classroom afterwards, a little boy remarked with fervour, 'Oh, comfortable, Miss, real comfortable'—a phrase which would, I feel sure, have enchanted the painter for it expressed the amplitude of Madame Manet's lap from the cat's point of view.

There had been a question on a collection of paintings by Degas. The question was, 'What do you think this painter was interested in most?' Quick as a flash, a fat boy with boot-button eyes put up his hand. 'Women, Miss.' 'Yes, that's quite right, but what about them?' Before I had time to finish my sentence the boy interrupted and said stolidly, 'Their movements, Miss.' I think the boy later became a butcher, but I like to think that perhaps he sometimes visits the Tate and looks knowledgeably and appreciatively at the paintings by Degas, and that he also sees feminine gestures through eyes enriched by Degas. We learnt that a number of the children had returned to the Tate on their own after this visit.

(3) The third aspect of the aim of education in and through painting is that the extension in observation and awareness enriches the pupil's vision and outlook and helps to widen his sympathies. This in turn often stimulates a desire to continue painting as a hobby in later life. As a teacher of painting one is of course primarily concerned with the ordinary person, not with the rare phenomenon of the budding painter. The genuine budding painter will be a painter anyway, but the potential appreciator of painting may, without the necessary encouragement, never develop these potentialities. I do not mean to suggest that every human being is potentially a lover of paintings, but rather that education should provide a means of developing the potentialities of those who can respond. Others will respond to other opportunities and develop other potentialities.

Summing up, the three-fold aim as it applied in England, was as follows:

(1) By painting pictures the pupil gained (*a*) understanding of the painter's function, and (*b*) an introduction to a non-materialist scale of value.

(2) This prepared him for critical appreciation of painting in general, and of the paintings in art galleries in particular.

(3) The activity of painting and studying paintings was one of the contributory factors in extending his observations, awareness and sympathies, of educating his emotions, and might prove a life-long interest or hobby.

How did this three-fold aim apply in Africa? Point (2) disappeared at once. You cannot appreciate what is not there and art galleries, if 5,000 miles away, cannot be seriously considered as a reality for the average African. There remained points (1) and (3).

We felt that point (1) could be retained as a conscious aim, though (*a*) would of course have a different significance in a country which had no painters or tradition of painting; (*b*) later appeared to exert a considerable influence.

Point (3), which we felt helped to justify the introduction of the subject into the curriculum, grew in importance as we continued our Art lessons. Its influence was felt in other subjects and spheres of school life.

It was unlikely, however, at the stage we had reached, that any African would continue painting as a hobby. Life outside school was not conducive to its encouragement. There might be a very few exceptions.

We had looked forward to introducing painting into the school, past experience had led us to believe that the subject had a universal and instant appeal, and we hoped to get a little light relief to balance our heavy burdens elsewhere. Various theories, mostly psychological, have been put forward to explain the peculiar fascination that painting pictures appears to have for children. I have taught all age-groups of European girls and boys, and from the most varied possible social backgrounds, urban and rural, but here again the reactions in African pupils were so different, so unpredictable, that they might have come from another world, as indeed they did. This also might have been foreseen had we had sufficient imagination ourselves but, in fact, African life was to us our 'Mobius strip'.

I had always warmly believed that all children, no matter of what race or creed, enjoyed some form of painting pictures if the teaching provided satisfaction with regard to achievement and imaginative expression. In the African school, in spite of approaching the subject with great caution, I was wholly unprepared for the complete indifference with which my efforts were met. As always, the pupils were docile and obedient and set about the job as they would have done had it been a problem of algebra or a question in geography. They were too polite to say anything but I felt that the painting business was accepted as part of the price paid for having a European headmistress.

The outstanding symptoms of this indifference were:

(*a*) The faces were completely mask-like and unmoved during painting lessons.

(*b*) At the end of the lesson, when paints and materials had been cleared away, not one single pupil ever glanced at his painting lying on his desk again, or ever looked sideways at anybody else's.

(*c*) When paintings were put on the classroom walls, I never found anybody looking at them.

(*d*) No child from another class ever looked in to see the paintings on the wall of the classroom next door.

(*e*) No-one ever asked a question about, or connected with, the painting.

(*f*) No African member of staff and no student training in the school, on any occasion, appeared to notice the existence of the paintings and certainly never made a single comment, favourable or otherwise. This may have been due partly to ignorance of what one 'ought to say' about painting; the teachers and students were no more familiar with painting than the pupils, but were sufficiently self-conscious not to want to expose themselves as 'ignorant'. Under the present system of education imposed on them and endured by them most Africans soon lose the lack of inhibitions which, to a great extent, they have when they come to school.

The remarkable feature in all this is the fact that at that stage there was never an exception. Not *one* child or adult behaved or reacted differently from the others.

In contrast to this situation I recalled the never-failing response, interest and controversy amongst European children and staff whenever a painting lesson was in progress or had taken place. I remembered how there were always some children who had to be dragged from their paintings and forcibly ejected from the room; how crowds of eager faces from other classes pressed against window-panes had to be shooed away. I remembered the never-ending arguments and discussions in classroom and staffroom and most of all I remembered the human relationships involved—the tough little boy who pulled me by my overall to see his painting and pointing with a paint-stained finger said, 'Them carrots look good, don't they? Real sweet carrots, they are'.

On one occasion, stung by the indifference, I tried to provoke some kind of response. There were three or four boys left in the classroom and I was feeling very inadequate and discouraged. 'Which painting do you like best?' I asked. Silently, without a flicker, and with a precise unanimity of timing that would have done credit to a well-organized parade ground, four hands were raised to indicate their own painting. They had not even glanced at any other. Perhaps I had completely lost all sense of humour, but that evening I seriously considered cutting out the painting lessons.

In the end it was a 'Deus ex machina' which gave the first fillip to the painting in the school and lit some sort of spark, and it was not at all an orthodox agent.

A Safety Week was being organized in the town and it

included a poster competition for African children at school. I knew that very few African schools indeed, and hardly any Junior Secondary Schools, included painting in their curriculum and though our pupils' paintings were raw and inexperienced I thought they might stand a chance as they would have very little to compete with. In the event, all their work appeared in the public exhibition and two of them won money prizes which were publicly awarded. This made a considerable impression and there were signs of a flickering interest in the age-group which had been involved in the competition.

The question concerning art which I used to be asked most frequently at home, in teachers' courses, talks to parents and public lectures, was 'What is it for?' My answer was always couched in terms of the three-fold aim already explained. The question was usually asked in all sincerity and a sincere question deserves sincere consideration and a sincere answer. I was always glad to be asked this particular question and certainly never resented it. No human being can be expected to take an interest in an activity which to him seems pointless.

After the slight prod given by the Safety Week competition I gave further thought to this question, and it now appeared to me that probably the biggest stumbling block to interest in the painting lessons had been this inability to see the point of it. This may sound very naïve, but it is a point which does not have to be considered when teaching European children (as opposed to adults) for the activity is usually enjoyed for its own sake and without question.

Now that at least two visible advantages had been perceived, namely money and a certain degree of prestige, there had been a dawning recognition that painting might lead to something practical for somebody. I want to make it clear that I make this statement without the slightest implication of criticism. If the reader interprets the statement to mean that the pupils were able to evaluate an activity only in terms of its material results, I would point out that that is how we all began our evaluations. The growing child evaluates his actions in terms of their returns. The difference was that our African pupils were wholly unsophisticated in regard to such an unfamiliar activity. What eventually developed during the next four years proved to us conclusively that African children no less than others are capable of disinterestedness in matters of creative work, and that painting helped them a good deal in arousing, appreciating and developing this non-materialistic sense of values.

It was about a year before pupils began to look at their own and at each others' paintings or to comment on them. I had included painting as one of the internal subjects for the Junior Secondary Leaving Examination and this also contributed to its being considered as an authentic 'subject'. Gradually other incidents helped to establish it. These were mostly connected with exhibitions organized through the auspices of the Society for Education through the Arts, in countries outside Uganda (England and Canada, for example) where the children's work aroused considerable interest and a knowledgeable response. This genuine and balanced appreciation from the outside world was one of the most vital influences in establishing a sense of confidence and self-respect in our pupils. It is not an exaggeration to say that one could almost see them acquiring some sort of 'poise' through this subject. I have sometimes watched when, for example, a boy of no outstanding gifts or personality, who had been painting for three years, came into the art room in his spare time to paint. It was almost as though he had left his usual personality outside the art room door, and with his carpentry apron (also often used to protect the clothes in painting lessons) had donned another. He appeared to have exchanged a tentative, rather drifting, gangling self, for a new self of quicker, neater, more purposeful movements, economical gestures, focused energies, and a facial expression of serene satisfaction. This wholly intangible transformation caused us to feel that we would willingly undergo again the bewildering gloom and depression of the first eighteen months.

What we did not realise was that we should never again experience quite the same difficulties or the same discouragement. Once interest and pride were aroused they were also, in some indefinable way, handed on. Whatever difficulties the younger inexperienced children might present to us, we had now acquired some experience and knowledge to deal with them, and, far more important even than that, we had the support and help of the older pupils in the school, as well as their paintings on the wall.

Another feature which helped us greatly was the building, after the first eighteen months or so, of an art and craft room so that besides the removal of physical difficulties, such as carting buckets of water into classrooms, a proper workshop atmosphere could be established. Pupils could paint in their spare time, art books could be left around for perusal, and objects of interest could be laid out for examination. I had always hoped to establish a link between painting and nature study, but unfortunately this was not possible as there were no teachers capable of the kind of imaginative approach it would have involved. We therefore did what we could inside the art room to foster on the one hand the observant eye, and on the other the desirable emotional attitude or feeling to accompany it. It is not the coldly observant eye one sets out to encourage, nor the sickly sentimental eye, but the alert eye ready to rejoice, to wonder and to observe with love as well as accuracy.

Wherever possible we illustrated aspects of some subject under discussion, which had some bearing on their painting; for example, 'Pattern in Nature' or 'Colour or Shapes in Nature', by putting out specimens of butterflies or shells (from the sea and the Lake), coloured leaves, skeleton leaves, leaf prints, and caterpillars. We used every opportunity to try to develop a feeling of wonder and sympathy in the children. This can only be done by example, by the way in which a teacher handles things and touches them and insists on their being handled, and so on.

Once more we came across apparently vast untapped

reservoirs of potentialities. It was a red-letter day when a boy cycled many miles in the pouring rain to my house, clutching in one hand a battered Yardley Lavender Talcum tin containing a somewhat squashed but still gaudy caterpillar which he excitedly delivered. The increased gentleness which the children showed towards living things also slowly became apparent, and wounded birds and other creatures were now usually brought to my office immediately.

Naturally this was not the result of the influence of any one subject (for I consistently used the time given to School Prayers as an opportunity to teach those desirable attitudes) but the painting lessons provided many extra opportunities for this. I once spent some time in Prayers on St. Francis of Assisi. In the art lesson we told the children how painters in the past had found various scenes from the life of St Francis, such as the pupils had just heard about, stimulating subject matter for paintings and we suggested that they too might care to try. We showed them a very small reproduction of Giotto's picture of St Francis feeding the birds. Giotto is a singularly appealing painter for African children to make contact with and they felt quite happy with even this tiny reproduction. They 'understood' it far better than any group of European children of their age group had done, though very much younger children in England, if unspoilt by the whole gamut of commercial and educational visual 'aids', reacted in much the same way. By this I mean that they immediately accepted the picture. There were no puzzled looks, no questions, no smiles of superior amusement such as one often meets in senior forms in England.

This brings us to the all-important matter of subjects and how to introduce and treat them. I had originally spent hours thinking about it, dithering between two theories. One held that children should be allowed to paint what and how they like; this is based on the unsound premise that every child is a hidden genius bursting to express himself in terms of painting. The other school of thought consisted of those who recoiled with precious horror at the very thought of the evils of 'influencing the children'.

However, I had discovered long before that films and comics rush in where teachers fear to tread, so I no longer had any scruples on that score. I had learnt the hard way that a teacher has to make up his mind as to what he believes to be right and wrong, good and bad, and must let his pupils see it. He cannot escape influencing them. He influences them by existing; whether his influence turns out to be negative or positive, it remains an influence. I was prepared to take the responsibility of influencing, and to risk the damage done, as I was more afraid of the nebulous, murky damage attending the non-influencing school of thought. But when I came to think this out as applied to African children, I did not feel so confident. Teachers and artists in England, whose opinions I greatly respected, reported having seen frightful 'Europeanized' paintings done by African children. I dreaded contributing to this despised category but, with no experience of teaching painting to African children, how could I guard against it? I had also seen examples of cheap illustration by African children, reminiscent of the work of pavement artists. This is not intended as a sneer against the pavement artist: his is a particular sphere. This, too, I wanted to avoid, but I felt far from smug about it for I was afraid of producing far worse things. On the other hand, I cherished no romantic fallacy that African children, if left to blossom alone, would automatically produce Altamira and Lascaux masterpieces. People clad in Manchester textiles, who bicycle to school, and who long to own a motor-car, a radio, and a burglar-proof house with glass windows, are no longer able to paint as if they lived in caves in the rocks, even if Uganda could provide the right kind of rocks. There was no putting the clock back; one could only go on.

Eventually I decided that I must accept the fact that I was a European and that any influence I could exert over my African pupils would inevitably be European. I would not waste any more time over the fruitless question of how to produce 'non-European-influenced' African art. I therefore concentrated on the more practical problem of finding suitable subjects for African children. Before launching into this question, however, I had better explain another problem peculiar to teaching painting in Uganda.

One of the first shocks we had was the realization that the number of colours which the children were *apparently* able to recognize was strictly limited. Indeed, in our ignorance, we at first even thought that there must be a considerable incidence of colour blindness. This supposition was soon proved completely false by application of the standard colour blindness tests, and by being introduced to the research done by Mr. K. Simon of Nairobi, who indicates that there appears to be less colour blindness among Africans than among Europeans.

By questioning the children as to what they called these colours in Luganda we quickly discovered what is, of course, well-known to anthropologists and people who have worked for any length of time with Africans, namely that there are very few words in the vernacular for colours, and that these are confined to colours involved in recognition of food and other things to do with sheer survival. For example, the words for yellow and ripe are related. It is difficult not to connect this with the fact that the banana or plantain, which is the staple food of the Baganda, is yellow when ripe (though it is cooked when it is green).

The English word 'blue' has now been taken into the Baganda's vocabulary as *bululu* though the word for black—*Ddugavu*—is still used for 'dark-blue' and 'dirty' and/or 'dark' in general. Once, staggered at the thought that for over 2,000 years, surrounded by the blue lake and the blue tropical skies, no Muganda[1] had apparently wished to refer to it, I asked for possible explanations of this from an African teacher. He did not see the point of the question and I then suggested that there was, after all, a utilitarian aspect to the blueness of

[1] *Muganda* is the singular form of *Baganda*.

the lake as it was associated with the serenity of the water and its concomitant safety for canoes. He replied, 'Oh, but we say something different for that', and produced a sentence meaning more or less that there would be no wind. One of the senior boys said to me when I had tried to discuss this same subject with him, 'But, Madam, we are not interested in colours'. That same boy is now, after four years, *very* interested in colours as he has developed a *Weltanschauung* which includes a different approach to the part that can be played by colour in the life of man.

It would be interesting to know whether any Muganda child during the last 2,000 years or so has ever lifted a questioning finger towards the lapis-lazuli lake or sky. Naturally, in the circumstances, it would get no further, but has the thought ever been born, to fade away unrecorded and unencouraged? It would be interesting to know what the first five hundred words of a Muganda child usually are, in what order they are normally acquired, and whether mostly as single words or very soon as phrases and sentences, affected perhaps by the part played in the language by elision. I have collected, with great difficulty, a short list in which there is some correlation between the vocabulary and such early drawings as I have been able to get hold of. There is an unexplored field of research here, the results of which would be of considerable interest and benefit to those genuinely interested in African children and in their proper, constructive education. The drawings of very young African children (6, 7, 8 years) suggest (though many more specimens would need to be collected) that the power symbols here in Uganda, the bicycle, and even more the motor-car, over-ride the emotional force and association of the home symbols, the hut or house and people (father, mother, and others). The very first scribbles of African children are even more difficult to get hold of because normally they have nothing to scribble with and if they draw at all they do so in the dust. Such evidence as I have been able to collect from later drawings indicates a preoccupation with legs. Continual reference to fatigue and tiredness also occurs in the older children's written work. Legs are almost always depicted grotesquely enlarged and with double lines, although the arms are hardly ever drawn with anything but single lines. I suspect that Europeans can form no remotely adequate conception of the drudgery and fatigue involved in the endless miles an African child is forced to walk, often carrying heavy burdens, often soaked to the skin and shivering with cold. Moreover, this walking must assume an importance and leave an impression proportionate to the corresponding lack of pleasant or comforting experiences to combat it, a compensation which exists for many European children who also have many miles to walk to school.

The Luganda word *myufu* is used to describe red, brown, maroon, pink, vermilion, crimson, scarlet, orange, mauve, lilac, purple, and other related colours. Such adjectives as 'vermilion' or 'crimson', for example, do not usually figure in the vocabulary of the 'man in the street' in England either, but in painting lessons in England, even if the children did not know the exact term for a different red, they would refer to it, for example, as 'a different red, Miss, a sort of pinky-yellow'. They would then badger the teacher to help them to manufacture the colour required. If the technical terms for the pigments were supplied, English children soaked these up like sponges, and in my experience I have rarely had to repeat them.

One of the first things we did in the school, therefore, was to make a simple chart of colours and their names. This chart included only black, white, grey, yellow, orange, vermilion, crimson-lake, green (viridian), blue (cobalt), pale-blue and dark-blue, mauve, and brown (raw umber). Some of the children had learnt the word 'purple' before coming to school and I did not at this stage fuss about the distinctions such as between mauve and purple. Later on we extended this chart to include shades of colours as well as a wider range of colour. We were less concerned with the technical names of the pigments which a painter would use, than with the terms which could be used to designate colours and qualities of colours in their English lessons, for example, lemon, turquoise, indigo, vivid green, lime (there are many limes in Uganda), bright orange, deep-blue. We put one of these charts in every classroom and I referred to it in English lessons and children soon got used to calling orange 'orange' and not 'red', pink 'pink' and not 'red', and mauve 'mauve' and not 'brown'. But this had by no means settled the question, as we later discovered.

During much later discussions with Africans, not only African teachers, after we had ourselves begun to learn Luganda, it transpired that the Baganda have a considerable variety of colour-names which apply specifically to the colours of cows, but these are best-known amongst the older generations of Africans and many of the younger generation have not learnt them. When I asked the reason for this, a very charming young Muganda said gloomily, 'Since you Europeans came, there are so many fewer cows'.

Returning now to the matter of subjects: as with English compositions, I had built up lists of subjects which had been carefully tried out and graded according to the points which they exercized, technical and otherwise. One of the most popular and successful first subjects with the middle school or senior boys in England was 'Portrait of a Clown' or 'Portrait of a Sailor', both of them clearly impossible in Uganda; so was the one for the girls, 'My Mother in her new hat'. Clowns and sailors are unknown and normally African women do not wear hats. In England the 'Clown' subject had, on several occasions, elicited the delighted remark from some member of the class, 'It's a good one this, isn't it, Miss, 'cos it don't matter about the face'. The cinema-imposed non-realistic ideal of 'handsomeness' produced some odd situations in England. In one class the boys gladly paid sixpence to the boy who they said 'could draw', for drawing their 'faces'. It is hardly necessary to add that the boy who could draw had achieved a facility of unbelievable slickness in reproducing the most nauseating likeness of film-stars from film magazines.

Our African pupils did not labour under the disadvantages of such vitiated vision or values.

I finally decided that 'Portrait of a Young African' would be my first subject. This would enable me to deal with the technique of engineering a single shape (that is, head and shoulders) inside the usual rectangle in the most economical and satisfactory way. It would also help the children to consider the painter's interest in human beings. The preliminary discussion would include my usual speech about not painting the faces 'black', and about faces not being geometrically spherical or square. I followed this up fairly soon by another portrait, 'Portrait of an Old Chief' or 'Portrait of an Old Country (or Peasant) Woman'. This produced some rather fetching pictures of old women smoking pipes, and old chiefs with gnarled hands. Naturally in the first instance the word 'portrait' had to be explained as nobody knew what it meant. We timed these portraits to coincide more or less with the compositions 'Portrait of my Mother' and 'Portrait of our Chief' or 'Portrait of my Grandfather (or Grandmother)' in the English lesson.

These lessons resulted in considerable extension of vocabulary and observation. The vocabulary charmed the children. 'Twinkling eyes', 'wrinkled/smooth', 'sticking-out ears', these were all received with signs of interest and enjoyment and entered rapidly into the vocabulary of their daily use. 'Go to the one with the sticking-out ears' you would hear a Prefect say with composure to a bewildered new arrival.

We did not dream at that time to what extent these portraits would capture the imagination and developing skill of our pupils; portrait painting eventually became one of the favourite pastimes of the older pupils. I am certain that this approach would encourage the emergence, within a few generations, of some noteworthy African portrait painters.

I had found that in teaching painting, as in teaching original writing, there were times when the introduction of a model to illustrate certain points and to set a standard, *not* to serve as something to be slavishly copied, produced noticeably beneficial results. Children are not born knowing the purpose and meaning of a portrait and its manifold aspects. The teacher must teach. (One of the most pernicious and phoney notions popularly entertained at home about this approach to teaching art is that it implies an *absence* of teaching.) In England I had found Van Gogh's portraits some of the most helpful. I used to hold up reproductions of a number of his portraits and ask the children to suggest titles for them. Frequently the titles suggested corresponded exactly with the titles given by the painter himself, which was the chief point of the exercise. 'Has the painter put this "person" across to us?' I remember one occasion when a boy in a London Primary School, on being confronted with Van Gogh's 'Portrait of an Actor' with its unmistakeable expression of specious persuasiveness, remarked with unadulterated shrewdness, 'That is a portrait of a teacher'. In Uganda, most of my carefully collected reproductions conveyed no meaning—Van Gogh's portrait of the Postman, for example, was useless as there are no postmen in Uganda. On the other hand, 'Head of a Boy', so aptly christened 'The Newspaper Boy' in London, did establish some contact with the African children as did also the various portraits of peasants, especially the old peasant. At a later stage, when the children already had some grasp of the 'language' of portrait painting, I found Modigliani's 'The Little Peasant', of which I had quite a large reproduction, was a useful picture to help the children to understand how essential it was for the painter to be in sympathy with and have knowledge and understanding of what he was painting. It was interesting here to see the effect of the children's environment on their reaction to the painting.

In England children had at once suggested:

(*a*) that the boy was a peasant or country-boy, or not a rich boy, because—

(*b*) his clothes were evidently his 'best clothes' though patched;

(*c*) he was not very used to wearing them because he looked uncomfortable in them;

(*d*) he had really outgrown them but could not afford to buy new ones, for example, the sleeves of his jacket were too short for him;

(*e*) his hands were the hands of a tiller of the soil.

The African children did not perceive these things by themselves but reacted with interest and appreciation when they were pointed out or elicited by questioning. Patched clothing conveys a different message to the ordinary Muganda African. It is not a matter of shame to wear rags because this means you have got another shirt or corresponding garment at home. If you wear patched or mended things this means you are very poor indeed as it indicates you have no alternative to wear; anything is better than to advertise such a pitiful state of affairs.

In case of misunderstanding about the use of reproductions I should like to stress that these were used in the discussions before painting, and were then removed. They were *not* copied. After the lesson they were left about where the children could study them for themselves and at their leisure if they were interested. I used reproductions to illustrate such points as the enormous difference and variety in backgrounds, or to show how some painters painted backgrounds to indicate the occupation or interests of the subject of the portrait, whereas others concentrated on the decorative possibilities. This helped to develop the children's understanding of the kind of freedom a painter enjoys and the kind of discipline he voluntarily submits to, the discipline of the rules which the materials and tools and subject matter of his craft impose upon him.

Slowly and laboriously, by trial and error, we built up a store of subjects which, judged by the results and gradually increasing participation of the pupils, seemed suitable for African children. These subjects included 'Myself under a tree', 'Looking after my father's cattle or goats', 'The Drummer' or 'Drumming',

'A hair-cut in the country' (it is common enough to see an open-air barber under a tree attending a customer seated on a rough chair, wooden box or petrol tin while those waiting chat in the sun), 'Fetching water' (from the well, spring, pond or local puddle), 'Washing clothes' (in the river, swamp, lake, etc.), 'Mother digging', 'Picking cotton', and a variety of others. For 'Character Portraits' we selected for continuous use from our try-outs, 'Portrait of a doctor (or nurse)', 'The Charcoal Seller', 'Portrait of a Sudanese Woman', 'The Beggar' (there are many crippled beggars), 'The Teacher', 'The Boy with the Pineapple', 'The Young Man with the Football', and so on. For practising purely decorative pattern we used the subjects 'A Fish' (a few dun-coloured varieties of fish from the Lake are sold in all local markets), 'A Butterfly', 'A Vase of Flowers' and some others.

This was all very well as far as it went, but we were rapidly brought to the conclusion that this was not very far for it soon became clear that the biggest obstacle in the way of progress was paucity of imagery. One cannot put into a picture what is not in one's head. We had so far stuck to the imaginative approach but when we first tried the subject 'A Vase of Flowers' we suffered a baffling disappointment. In spite of the introductory discussion on the variety of shapes, colours and textures of flowers, the paintings produced were almost all merely a collection of scribbles on stalks (single-lined). I had very occasionally encountered one of these in England but I had never in fifteen years met with almost a whole set of them. As this was usually one of the best subjects, I was not prepared to give in and let it go without further investigation.

After every failure we used to sit down and think exhaustively about what might have been some of the causes. We had by this time dealt, seemingly satisfactorily, with the worst of the 'colour problem', though we still tended to get sporadically, and often in our eyes unaccountably, paintings in 'dirty colour' as we used to do in the first months. On the whole, however, we were getting good clean colour (we used mostly powder paint) often in Gauginesque combinations which delighted our jaded European eyes. (Our pupil's colour sense had not been ruined by the Ostwald colour wheel or similar gadgets and theories.) We had achieved nothing so satisfactory with regard to shapes. These seemed to fall into two sharply defined categories:

(1) The shapes which the children 'knew', that is, cattle, goats, banana trees, huts, etc., and which they tackled without the slightest hesitation. Such drawings were only to a certain extent abstracted and they conveyed the same feeling of authenticity as the rock paintings so yearned after by nostalgic Europeans. I was strongly reminded of Eric Newton's comment on the Altamira bison, 'It is emphatically not a diagram of a mind-image. It is a descriptive record of a momentary pose observed with the swiftness of a snapshot.'[1] I am not sure about the word 'observed'. It is something which is better described by the word 'known' than 'observed'. Observation must presumably come into it somewhere, but unconsciously. The African child has seemingly absorbed the image of a cow, numberless images of cows in characteristic positions and similarly a banana tree, but they are not mind-images in the usual sense of the word, nor are they so much the product of things seen as of things felt. They have less to do with the visual than with the kinaesthetic and the tactile. Like the complicated rhythm beaten out by the musicians on the xylophone or drum, they are not consciously produced; these rhythms are performed with bodily movements while the eyes of the performers are gazing elsewhere, like a knitter knitting a complicated pattern while reading a book.

(2) The second category of shapes consisted of those to which we had drawn the children's attention, and here most unpredictable things occurred, governed mainly, I think, by a feeling on the part of the pupils that shapes of such things as flowers were of supreme unimportance. They had never been observed.

[1] Eric Newton, *European Painting and Sculpture*, p. 47 (1941).

When I asked them to paint a butterfly, stressing the decorativeness of the patterns on butterfly wings and their shapes (there are many graceful swallow-tailed varieties in Uganda), I got a set of square butterflies; each one had two wings decorated with geometric patterns. (The deep-rooted geometric pattern of primitive peoples is illustrated in their handwork, such as bead-work or plaiting.) In England I had, of course, also had two-winged, though very rarely square, butterflies (this, by the way, is by no means correlated with town dwelling as might be imagined) but never a complete set with no exception. The lack of exceptions in all these occurrences dismayed us, though if we had been anthropologists or social psychologists presumably we would have been more prepared for it.

Pattern in most unsophisticated communities is geometric. It is the unsophisticated labourer's wife who puts the china dogs one on either side of the mantelpiece, as Norman Callan once pointed out.[1] Such traditional pattern as was to be found locally in Uganda is also geometric. Hence, in the example above, we had been presented with pattern unconnected with any observation of butterflies.

On the next occasion, after the failure of 'The Vase of Flowers', when I tried this subject again with another class I actually took in a number of flowers and leaves and grasses. I expatiated on their differences, the difference of their 'personalities'; the fat, heavy, robust zinnia with its glowing colours and stiff markedly characteristic leaves; the light, dancing, feathery cosmos, etc. I handed the flowers around. I insisted on the children touching and handling them. This time there was a marked improvement in the result. There was greater variety, greater feeling for texture, definite shapes to the flowers—that is definite outlines, not undefined scribbles. I tried again with another class, took in the flowers, but was pushed for time and did not pass them round to be handled. There was a noticeable falling off in results. I discussed the

[1] Norman Callan, *Poetry in Practice*, p. 24 (1938).

matter with my colleague. She had also noticed that seeing without touching produced either much weaker results or sometimes no results, whereas whenever the children handled something there seemed to be a corresponding improvement.

These observations coincided and overlapped with observations made in other spheres of school activity, such as those of the children's reactions to films and filmstrips already mentioned in other chapters. It seemed more than ever likely that the African children had different eye habits from European children and that the whole question of how and what an African child sees is an extremely complex one of which we are very (if not wholly) ignorant. This ignorance is not a matter for complacency, and the problem will not yield its secrets to a flood of European-conceived 'visual aids'. It requires to be investigated systematically with the utmost circumspection and sympathy. We pored over J. Z. Young's fourth Reith Lecture.[1] The extracts which we felt were particularly relevant to our problem seem to me to be of such significance that I shall quote them here.

. . . 'The brain of each one of us does literally create his or her own world.' Young then explains this, illustrating his explanation with reference to the new-born child and certain cases of congenitally blind people whose sight is restored. He shatters the romantic idea that this is an immediately pleasant experience. 'The patient in opening his eyes for the first time gets little or no enjoyment; indeed, he finds the experience painful. . . . He has no conception of a space with objects in it, although he knows all about objects and their names by touch.' We are told it will take years for the patient to learn to use his physical sight to 'see'; the reason is that,

> . . . His brain has not been trained in the rules of seeing. We are not conscious that there are any such rules; we think that we see, as we say, 'naturally'. But we have in fact learned a whole set of rules during childhood. [Young quotes the following example] . . .

[1] J. Z. Young, 'The Establishment of Certainty' in *Doubt and Certainty in Science* (1951).

'one man when shown an orange a week after beginning to see said that it was gold. When asked 'What shape is it?' he said, 'Let me touch it and I will tell you.' After doing so, he said that it was an orange. Shown next a blue square, he said it was blue and round. When the angles were pointed out to him he said, 'Ah. Yes, I understand now, one can *see* how they feel'.

When I first read this I was astounded because so much of our experience with African children appeared analogous. The predominance of their tactile responses was continually attracting our attention. Frequently their hands seemed to 'tell' them more than their eyes. Furthermore, Professor Young's statement that, 'The patient often finds that the new sense brings only a feeling of uncertainty and he may refuse to make any attempt to use it unless forced to do so. *He does not spontaneously attend to the detail of shapes.* He has not learned the rules. . . . ' again appeared to us analogous because the African, brought into contact with so many new experiences, presented from so many new angles, also exhibited, we thought, a similar feeling of uncertainty or insecurity. He had not learnt the European rules.

As with Professor Young's patient . . . 'It is not that all along the eyes or brain were incapable of acting normally. What these people lack is the store of rules in the brain—rules usually learnt by the long years of exploration with the eyes during childhood.' Without wishing to strain the analogy too far, we felt that there was a parallel between the difficulties of Professor Young's patient and many Africans whose problems seemed also deeply affected by the matter of selection and the 'lack of store'. Young points out that children select the significant features of visual experience and produce appropriate words and other motor responses, and that a normal person learns the rules of seeing by connecting parts of the sensory input with motor acts that lead to satisfaction, for instance naming and the fulfilment of communication.

We do not know exactly what happens to the brain as it learns to react to shapes during that period of training. At first the eyes wander at random over the visual field. *Probably learning to move the eyes in certain ways is an important part of the process . . .*

. . . So we can believe that the brain gradually comes to act in certain special ways. One of the earliest of these habits gives us a tendency for the eye to sweep along lines instead of in all directions at random.

The eye habits of members of a society are 'learned'; they are largely governed by the satisfaction they afford the viewer, and their purpose is largely selective. There appear to be no grounds for the assumption that African children have the same eye habits as European children. This difference in eye habits affects many aspects of the education of Africans by Europeans. Chinese children read, for example, from the top to the bottom and from right to left. The African child has presumably the potentiality for either, but what we do not know with any certainty is the nature of the eye habits he has acquired before he comes to school, and how these differ from what we imagine them to be. The result of our ignorance is that we expect and demand from him responses which only confuse him.

In view of these considerations we now determined to embark on a course which is regarded as a heresy by the rabid supporters of the theory that children should only paint 'from imagination' (that is, that they should only paint 'out of their heads'). This is, of course, in any case, only one kind of imaginative painting and depends for its success (if success means satisfaction to the painter as well as to the beholder) not only on what is in the head, including store of images, but also on knowing what to do with it. Presumably even the most fanatical of the 'from imagination only' theorists would not claim that Van Gogh's sunflowers or Cezanne's apples were unimaginative, yet we know very well how the artists set about painting these. I always remember with pleasure the story of how at the one hundred and fifty-seventh sitting Cezanne said to his sitter, a distinguished personage who was having his portrait painted, 'I am not displeased with the shirt front'. It is well to remember that human beings were not made to fit theories. I once asked a painter whose works are in the Tate how he had painted the still life of quinces which was still on his easel. He hesitated for a second and then said with great charm, 'It is a portrait of each quince'. On the other hand, a boy in a voluntary art class in England, which I had taught consistently for six years, used to look appreciatively at the groups of flowers, fruit, and other objects which I set up from time to time for those who wanted to paint them, but he did not attempt to paint them himself. Once there was a particularly lush group and he was the first in the room. He gazed at it with his hands in his pockets and said, 'Gosh, that's a smashing still life', and then added rather wistfully, with a sigh and considerable perspicacity, 'but I paint better out of my head', which was true.

The all-important principle is to preserve flexibility so that each individual child is given a chance to achieve skill and satisfaction along his own lines. This is impossible if any one theory is rigidly adhered to. Dangerous and wasteful as this is in England, it is infinitely more so in Africa, where the African children have no kind of defence against such aggressive theorists and where the resulting damage is likely to be more far-reaching and permanent.

Uganda is a country of blazing, dazzling colours, particularly rich in magentas, scarlets, orange, indigo and purples. It is uncompromising in its lights and darks, and shadows almost assume solidity and spread patterns with the edginess of a stencil. Every richly varied shape is in some sharp juxtaposition of either colour, tone or texture. The course we decided to embark on was to exploit these factors to the utmost, and to try at the same time to arouse a justifiable pride in the children in the glowing treasures of their country; we also hoped to learn something about the children's potential, and their development with regard to shape and line.

We therefore brought in a mass of fruit and vegetables from the market and timed it to coincide with the English composition 'A Visit to the Market', for which the model was an extract from D. H. Lawrence's *Sea and Sardinia.* The first thing that transpired was that the children did not know what half the things were called in the vernacular. This was partly because many of the things were only eaten by Europeans; but this was not entirely the case, as there were violent arguments as to what they really did call the things they ate themselves. The children were always interested in European food and its preparation—though I never did manage to give a satisfactory explanation of sausages.

This combined exercise of English and painting proved very valuable indeed, specially to us teachers; the handling of the objects was of the greatest importance. We repeated this exercise every year and always with the same favourable results; it made this study of flowers, fruit and vegetables combined with jugs, bowls, coloured tea-cups (in fact all the appurtenances of a still life) part of the permanent core of our art lessons. With it we tried to instil and encourage in the children the twin principles of reverence for life and of being true to their own truth, that is their own interpretation of what they experienced. We tried to inculcate the dictum of Leonardo da Vinci, 'Falsehood is so utterly vile that though it should praise great works of God, it offends His divinity. Truth is of such excellence that if it praise the meanest things they become ennobled'.[1]

There was a marked increase in interest and an encouraging improvement in the painting, particularly with regard to shape, but what now began to emerge was the ability to express what must have been present in the children all the time, a rather unusual—by European standards—susceptibility to texture. We did not, of course, exclude paintings 'out of one's head' but alternated them with paintings of things observed and studied. There was a more than hoped-for carry-over to the paintings 'out of one's head', thus supporting us in the belief that the main lack had been of imagery. These imaginative

[1] Leonardo da Vinci, *Notebooks,* Vol. 1, p. 84 (1938).

compositions now became far more lively, furbished with far greater detail, supplied spontaneously by the pupils without suggestion from the teacher. There was even, rare as a pearl of great price, a hint of humour. Suggestion was now greatly reduced although some was still necessary, varying in degree with each pupil.

Greatly cheered by this we became more abandoned and less inhibited about painting things looked at, and introduced more and more 'looking at things' and touching them.

Though we still did portraits from imagination as before (for instance, 'Portrait of my Father') we now asked every boy to face his neighbour and paint 'Portrait of the Boy opposite me'. We produced mirrors and did self-portraits. These were easily the most popular and were taken very seriously indeed. For us they were revealing in more ways than one, for they often reflected characteristics in the painter, which we had previously overlooked or had not taken into account. Despite certain understandable vanities the pupils mostly displayed an enviable detachment with regard to recording their features, and the characteristic expression was nearly always caught.

We revived the subject 'Myself under a tree' but preceded it by an exercise based on our more recent experiences. The stereotyped 'cabbage-tree' so often drawn by European children was not produced by our pupils; they tend to produce things like baobab trees (though in this district they had not usually seen these). Our pupil's trees had a very square trunk and branches more like roots at the top. Our pupils had painted some singularly dead-looking trees in their first attempts. We now made drawing-pads the size of a quarter of a page of *The Times*, and armed with these and pen and ink, we took the children out and introduced them to six different trees—a lemon tree, an acacia, a magnolia, a wild fig, a cypress, and a flame tree. We pointed out a seventh, one we did not know by name, but which had singularly decorative leaves. We made them touch the trunks of all of them, we picked the leaves, examined the buds and the flowers of the flowering ones, drew their attention to the outline of the trees, and then let them pick out four to make sketches of. They could make as many sketches as they liked. I had also made black silhouettes of some of these trees and put them up in the art-room as 'tree-shapes'. I told the children how Van Gogh had said that if you are going to paint a tree you must enter into the spirit of a tree, you must breathe like a tree, feel the wind in your hair, and feel the moonlight on your limbs, you must *be* a tree. This called forth an unexpected response, of solemn eyes, affectionate smiles and nods, and sounds of approval. From then on, the trees in our paintings began to breathe a little.

I had carefully avoided the painting of single sprays of flowers or single plants, on account of my own dismal experiences at school, where we were forced to copy a nasturtium or, much worse, a rose, in a manner that failed to be either botanical or artistic. (These are not necessarily mutually exclusive, as Edward Wilson's drawings and paintings demonstrate.) It seems worth while quoting an incident which a good many years ago concerned a pupil of mine, whose previous art teacher had trained all her pupils in this meticulous 'copying'. On one occasion the pupil had been faced with a rose which had been partly consumed by a caterpillar. This gnawed piece she conscientiously copied, doing her best to indicate every mark of tooth or claw. The drawing came back from the teacher, who had collected the drawings for 'marking', with a whole philosophy of life succinctly expressed in the comment, 'Do not include blemishes'.

Some years ago in England I had been much impressed by the inspired way in which a London art teacher had introduced and tackled the painting of single sprays of flowers or single plants. The approach was very different from that of 'exact copying' and I now felt it would be worth while trying this new approach with our African pupils. The exercise proved fruitful but once more raised the elusive question of colour recognition and its relation to language. One of the plants painted with an older group of boys was a heavy vermilion canna. We talked about it first as usual, but one of the boys painted the flower brown or near-brown. He was an intelligent boy but I did not think he was consciously choosing to paint the canna brown for artistic reasons. I therefore asked him, 'Did you mean to paint it that colour?' He looked at me in astonishment. I asked him to bring his bun-tray of pigments close to the actual canna. I then said, 'Which colour in the tray do you think is like the canna?' He looked first at the canna, then into the tray and after a moment's hesitation he pointed to the vermilion, *not* the umber he had used. I said 'But you haven't used that colour, all the same, have you? Did you *mean* not to? Didn't you want to use it?' He still looked surprised, and rather bewildered, and murmured, *myufu*. Since the Luganda word *myufu* means both brown and red and also covers crimson and vermilion, one cannot help considering whether African children do not to some extent paint linguistically. I suspect that what had happened was that the boy had looked at the canna, had said to himself *myufu*, and as this is most closely associated with brown, had then gone from the word to the brown pigment in the bun-tray. Then, without looking much more at the canna, had turned to the charcoal sketch of his flower and painted it *myufu*. He was in fact painting through *the word*, not through the eyes. I questioned him, but he could not explain and I did not wish to confuse him any further.

Later I came across further evidence of this linguistic painting in the primary school. Here also I taught the English names of the basic colours and put up a chart in the classroom. I asked the children to make up sentences using these colours. A number wrote 'My grandmother's hair is blue'. When asked to point out on the chart the colour they thought their grandmother's hair really was a minority pointed to the blue square with perfect confidence. Others giggled and pointed to the black (or grey) square. Grey they found very difficult. This also throws light on blue faces and blue trees in the painting lessons.

We had other indications of similar confusions apparently related to language, but this is clearly a subject which would repay careful and systematic investigation. Teaching an average of 35 periods a week left us no time in which to do anything systematic or organized with our discoveries. It was all we could do to make notes on them in order to remember them correctly.

We had set ourselves an aim, and in four years, after the initial period of great discouragement, we felt that there was ample evidence to show that this aim was justified, and that with our pupil's co-operation we had evolved an approach that might help to lead to those 'good states of mind' which Clive Bell has pointed out, 'alone are good as ends'[1] and which one of the most deeply religious painters who has ever lived has movingly described in one of his letters to his brother:

Dear Theo,

... I think that everything that is really good and beautiful, of inward moral, spiritual, and sublime beauty in men and their works, comes from God, and that all that is bad in men and their works is not God, and God does not approve of it. But always think that the best way to know God is to love many things. Love a friend, a wife, a something, whatever you like, but one must love with lofty and serious intimate sympathy, with strength, with intelligence, and one must always try to know deeper, better and more. ... To try to understand the real significance of what the great artists, the serious masters, tell us in their masterpieces, that leads to God. One man has written or told it in a book, another in a picture. Well, think much and think all the time, that unconsciously raises your thought above the ordinary level.[2]

If we had contributed only a little towards helping our African pupils to 'love many things', 'always to try to know deeper, better and more', and to 'think much and think all the time', because that unconsciously raises one's thoughts above the ordinary level, we might consider ourselves much privileged.

[1] Clive Bell, *Civilisation*, p. 86 (1928).

[2] 'Dear Theo' in *Van Gogh*, edited by Irving Stone.

GENERAL CONCLUSIONS

With special reference to teacher training

> Never was it more necessary than it is today to relate our philosophy to the conditions of a rapidly changing world. And never was it more necessary to refer our techniques to the ultimate ends for which they should be used.[1]

In a country like Uganda there will almost inevitably be an increasing tendency to impose techniques of instruction in the classroom and in the training college. This will have equally inevitable repercussions in the field of language teaching.

A student from a European or other well-established country, already educated in the tradition of his own people, can confidently demand specific techniques for specific purposes as a time-saving device. But if a mechanistic approach is to take the place of imaginative education in and through language in schools, and is to become the universal approach in a young unfolding country like Uganda, then the implications are grave and the inhabitants of the country, especially parents and teachers, should be aware of them.

The teaching of English to foreigners is often viewed from two different angles which form a curious paradox. Not infrequently both views are held, also paradoxically.

The one view sees the English language and the teaching of it as a kind of mystique. This theory is largely engendered and supported by certain teachers of English, and English educationists, but generally arouses the scepticism of teachers of other modern European languages, or foreign teachers of English in other European countries. According to this mystique, English is a language far too subtle, complex and elusive to submit to any of the various and, it is implied, crude teaching techniques which have been found successful in teaching other European languages. English therefore acquires a kind of aura

[1] M. V. Jeffreys, *Personal Values in the Modern World* (1962).

which it is considered vulgar, if not blasphemous, to attempt to penetrate. Why exactly English should be so wholly different from all other European languages, considering its origins, is never fully explained. Many staffrooms are familiar with the battle between the English teacher who supports this myth and the Modern Language teacher, who, harassed by his responsibilities, points out tartly that if he had not already done the language-teaching part of the English teacher's job, the latter and his pupils would find themselves in something of a predicament.

The other view sees all language-teaching in terms of techniques and skills. It embodies the notion that sufficient techniques or skill guarantee mastery of any language. This approach is in direct opposition to all *Gestalt* conceptions of education, and forcibly reminds me of an enthusiastic art teacher I encountered a good number of years ago, who had started an adult art class. With commendable keenness she reported that she insisted on her pupils drawing forty-five elbows, knees, shoulders, etc., so that when finally they were allowed to attempt to assemble these physical items and to draw a living figure, they would be well-equipped with the skills essential to the success of this exacting task. I met her again later, and asked whether the figures had ever come to life. She replied mournfully that she just could not understand why it was that when the elbows and arms, knees and legs had eventually been assembled, something vital still seemed to be missing.

From the experience of teaching at the Primary and Secondary school level and also at adult level in Y.W.C.A. classes, I reached the following conclusions:

(1) The substitution of instruction in techniques for imaginative education is one of the greatest dangers to African development—if this development is to be anything more than the acquisition of a superficial veneer.

(2) A great deal of research is needed, not in the first instance aiming to establish techniques but concerned primarily with the study of the perceptions and imagery of

African children, so that such techniques as are required can evolve from a study of the human being they are to serve. For example, if tactile and auditory responses are found to be more acute than the visual, then methods of teaching should take cognizance of this and be adjusted accordingly. At the same time, other methods to encourage and develop the potentialities of the weaker responses, such as the visual, need to be devised.

(3) In connection with the question of imagery, special research is needed into the vernacular and its bearing on concepts and imagination. It is impossible to overestimate the importance of this.

'Facts are unlike to speakers whose language background provides unlike formulation of them.'[1]

'There is no one metaphysical pool of universal thought. Speakers of different languages see the Cosmos differently, evaluate it differently, sometimes not by much, sometimes widely. Thinking is relative to the language learned. There are no primitive languages.'[2]

The last statement should be borne in mind by all who contemplate a policy which involves the extermination, whether abruptly or gradually, of a people's mother tongue, or the introduction of such measures in education as the teaching of reading and writing to African children in English instead of in their mother tongue.

Consideration of the far-reaching effects of such a policy should not be lightly ignored; on the one hand it can engender a most undesirable language snobbery, while on the other hand its offensive and wounding implications may arouse the kind of burning resentment which eventually finds expression, not unjustifiably, in equally offensive forms.

When such measures as those just indicated are contemplated, two main excuses are often offered in explanation and defence. The first is that the indigenous population has asked

[1] Benjamin Whorf, *Language, Thought and Reality*, M.I.T.

[2] *Ibid.*, Foreword by Stuart Chase.

for them. In the case of Africans who desperately desire to acquire a good standard of English, it is quite comprehensible that they should ask for English to be started as soon as possible, or 'from the beginning' in Primary Schools. Many Africans take the ingenuous quantitative approach. They do not realize the two gravest concomitants of such a policy, which are: (*a*) if the quality of English teaching at the present time (that is 1963) seems inadequate and is, in fact, responsible for some of the worst features of the Africans' spoken and written language, then increasing the quantity—say, four years' dubious English teaching to six or eight years—would only decrease the chances of the African child ever acquiring correct or fluent English later; (*b*) the psychological consequences of a measure which deprives a child of his mother tongue at a crucial stage in his development is likely to have as yet unestimated and unanticipated repercussions. Moreover such a child's teacher, who also has difficulties with his English, will also suffer.

Young African children on first coming to school already have many adjustments to make of a nature very different from European children. The emotional associations they will form when first introduced to the basic skills will have a lasting effect on their sentiments and attitudes. To deprive a child of the comfort and security afforded by the homely familiarity of the mother tongue at a time when he is most in need of reassurance and confidence would seem not merely to be contrary to all scientifically established psychological and educational principles, but surely contrary also to all human conceptions of a child's deepest needs.

Many Africans, new as they are to formal education, cannot appreciate the implications of such measures; Europeans in the full guilt of knowledge and experience, can. We do not usually say, 'I gave my child a drink of arsenic because he wanted to see what it tasted like'.

The second excuse which is offered, and which is a sounder one, is the factor of the difficulties involved in schools where a number of different tribes and dialects are represented. A common language and medium of instruction is required. Here it would seem possible and better to choose one of the leading vernaculars and to make that the medium of instruction, rather than anything so hopelessly alien as a European language. By the same law an English child attending an Infants' school, and somehow deprived of English as his medium of instruction, would find it less disconcerting to be taught in French or German than in Luganda. The time required to accustom oneself to a language allied to one's own is much less[1] than with a language completely alien, however useful the latter may be. Also, the psychological and linguistic adjustments are far less exacting. From an educational point of view, it is the long-term policy that matters. We might remember the inspiring example of the Pestalozzi children's village in Switzerland, where such a careful balance is preserved and cherished between the mother-tongue and the acquired language, and where the young children are all taught in their mother tongue. The administrative difficulties may be great, but surely with vision and skill they should not prove insuperable, and the reward in terms of human happiness and good would surely be worth the struggle. (This will inevitably prove to be a forlorn hope.)

(4) It should be recognized that successful performance in examinations means no more than successful performance. It does not substitute European imagery for African imagery, for example. In the case of the School Certificate class studying the 'Lady of Shalott' (mentioned in chapter 1) twenty-seven out of twenty-nine passed in English Literature, and seventeen of them obtained credits, and their results in English Language were above the average for the country. This in no way alters

[1] It would seem to be weeks as opposed to years. The Principal of a Teacher-Training College with a school attached in Tanganyika estimated that Bantu children from non-Swahili-speaking tribes became fluent in Swahili in a matter of weeks. For children from non-Bantu tribes it would probably be necessary to provide boarding schools for them and to staff them with their own teachers for the youngest age-groups, as has been done in the Pestalozzi schools.

the fact of the pupils' imaging Sir Launcelot as a large and impressive Muganda in war regalia, and the Lady of Shalott as living on an island in Lake Victoria; nor does it prevent anybody from getting a credit. Why should it? The examiner also translates his candidates' answers into terms of his own imagery. It might be apposite to quote an instance which occurred when a visiting Professor of Statistics from the U.S.A. asked a group of third year sociology students the following question: 'If the statement "All Americans are rich" is not true, what statement is true?' Not one student could suggest such a statement. The Professor was somewhat shocked, as he had before him a group of students selected by European examination results, but success in European examinations does not make an African into a European; and Western ways of thinking which have evolved throughout the centuries remain enigmatic. They are doubly mysterious when couched in this second language which has been acquired by means of European techniques.

(5) Through the emphasis on techniques the specific and vital needs of African children and teachers in Uganda schools may well be neglected and their potentialities ignored, with inevitable repercussions in other spheres of living. This will be particularly apparent in the policy pursued with regard to teacher-training. Sir Richard Livingstone has pointed out the dangers that beset a country when people become so engrossed with 'educational machinery' (such as providing schools) that they no longer properly consider what is to be taught inside them.

> Machinery is indispensible to education, but when it has been provided the bigger problem of education remains and begins. What are we to do? At what should education aim? What sort of human beings should it produce? These questions might interest us more. . . . Knowledge is important, still more so is the power to use it; but most important of all is what man believes, what he thinks good and bad, whether he has clear values and standards and is prepared to live by them. Paradox as this may sound, this matters

more to the making of a new world[1] and to its preservation, even than equality of opportunity. But of this all-important side of education—doubly important in a world of shaken beliefs and uncertain values—we hear very little. Speeches, conferences, the educational press are more occupied with educational machinery than with education. . . . As Plato said the noblest of all studies is the study of what man should be and how he should live. It is also the most important of all studies; do we give it enough attention?[2]

The urgent question in Uganda is just how much attention is given to it in the training of her teachers. All branches of art have to do with selection and interpretation, and teaching is an art and the teacher is an artist. It is the teacher's responsibility to select from the vast panorama of human knowledge and experience and to interpret what he has selected to his pupils. The sensitivity with which the selection is made and the quality of the imagination permeating the interpretation is the measure of the stature of the teacher as an artist. This applies equally, if not more, to the teacher of teachers, and it is precisely here in the sphere of the training of teachers that some vision and imagination is required.

Two objections are invariably raised.

The first is the old argument of expediency. Quantity before quality; as many teachers are needed it does not matter if they can teach, or what they teach, as long as they are in the classroom. They may even be found only spasmodically in the classroom, but they add to the number of teachers on the school's pay-sheet. The growth in the number of teachers and schools looks pleasing as a graph and happily gives no indication of quality. It should, however, be borne in mind, especially by parents, that a teacher is an influence for good or bad, and the children are not files, impervious to influence. The comfortable and quantitative graph showing the educational 'progress' made, in terms of the increase in numbers of teachers and classrooms, in no way compensates for the damage which

[1] In this case a new Uganda.

[2] Sir R. Livingstone, *Education for a World Adrift* (1944).

may be done to young human lives, by those teachers whose chief function is to improve the appearance of the graph.

The second argument is one which is even more frequently heard and is not without its parallel in England. This is the argument that blames the material. It is no good, so goes the argument, to talk high-falutin', non-realistic nonsense about an imaginative or liberal approach to teaching and the training of teachers, when the teachers in training are as they are. With such material, it is maintained, there is only one thing to do and that is to give them a cast-iron syllabus, constructed and thought of in cast-iron terms with cast-iron methods and prescribed text-books, and make them toe the line. This cynical approach is not wholly incomprehensible. It arises partly out of a legitimate dislike of inefficient muddle. Unfortunately rigidity is only another form of inefficiency with a tidier appearance.

In reply to both arguments I should like to begin with a quotation from a report of the conference on Teacher Training held at Nairobi in August 1956, through the instigation of the Advisory Council on African Education and the Christian Council of Kenya. The report was the result of an invitation to Mrs. K. M. Williams, then Principal of Whitelands Training College, Putney, to visit Kenya and study and advise on the organization of teacher training by Protestant Missions.

The school text-book is too often the only source of information for students and forms their sole subject of study. There are exceptions to this procedure, particularly in relation to practical subjects, but it must be said that in general the teaching given to students is mechanical and stereotyped. They are told precisely what they must learn, what they must teach and how they must teach it. *Such a process must stifle interest and initiative, and put a premium on verbal learning at the expense of understanding. It does not discriminate between the able student, who could contribute ideas of his own, and the less gifted,* who needs individual help to achieve a grasp of the ideas he will have to impart. It can be accepted that a teacher with poor general education will need more definite guidance on teaching methods than one who has a broad knowledge of his subject.

What should be changed is the assumption that all training needs to be of this illiberal kind. The two fundamental parts of a teacher's formal preparation are the continuation of his own education and the study of children's behaviour and ways of learning. (This means, of course, *African* children's behaviour and *African* children's ways of learning.) If these foundations are well laid teaching methods can be developed which are sound and flexible. Where an enterprising member of a College staff has attempted to stir the imagination of students so that they can anticipate the responses of children to a proposed lesson, some very lively and effective teaching has been achieved.[1] [My italics.]

No-one would deny that the students of very limited knowledge and ability will need to be taught what to teach and shown how to teach it, nor that a large proportion of students are, in fact, of very limited knowledge and ability and that this is probably even an understatement. The objection to the two arguments described is their sweeping absoluteness and the abuses to which they lead in practice. The arguments leave no room, as Mrs. Williams has pointed out, for discrimination between the able student with imaginative potentialities and the average and below-average student. In England in a two-year training college it was possible to find in each batch of 100 students six or eight who would respond to the more imaginative forms of teaching and training and who would leave the college with a contribution of their own to make to the teaching profession. This was well worth all the trouble and energy one could put into their course. The rest would assimilate what they could, and most would go out and preserve the *status quo*, and if they had a sensible and sympathetic attitude to children they would be doing an honourable job at that. I do not think it exaggeratedly optimistic or unrealistic to expect to find among every hundred African students training to be teachers, a handful who would be able to respond to the same stimulus and challenge as those in England. The charge of being unrealistic or worse must be brought against those who maintain that nothing can be done to relax the cast-iron

[1] The content of the courses, Paragraph 12. 36/17/109.

approach to training until there are considerable numbers of able and imaginative students to merit a different approach. There never will be. Moreover they are not to be found in anything but very limited numbers in any country, for the simple reason that imaginative and able young people climb Everest, work in laboratories and hospitals, man ships and aeroplanes, and some of them teach. What seems a monstrous injustice and heart-breaking stupidity is that this hypothetical handful of students out of every hundred in Uganda, through whom all pioneer and imaginative work in education should develop, are at present (1963) not only neglected but forced into the mould admittedly prepared for those of a totally different calibre.

Moreover, *all* students, of whatever ability, need to be taught what to teach and shown how to teach it. Once again it is the quality of imagination in the approach and methods suited to the different grades of students that is in question. From my own contact with students in training and with trained teachers during my years in Africa one thing emerges as certain. Here is a potential as yet ungauged and untapped which could be developed imaginatively in the service of the African children of Uganda. But this can only be attempted if we are prepared to approach the matter with the humility proper to the artist in the face of his material, frankly admitting our ignorance. We must not come with a mind stuffed with preconceived ideas of what Africans can or cannot do, or of what they like or do not like; nor must we try to impose European techniques on the African student in training whether he likes it or not. What is needed is not the imposing of sameness but research to illumine differences, those differences which constitute the richness of life and of peoples.

Our educational policy is based on two enormous fallacies. The first is that which regards the intellect as a box inhabited by autonomous ideas, whose numbers can be increased by the simple process of opening the lid of the box and introducing new ideas. The second fallacy is that all minds are alike, and can profit by the same system of training. All official systems of education are systems of pumping the same knowledge by the same methods into radically different minds. Minds being living organisms, not dustbins, irreducibly dissimilar and not uniform, the official systems of education are not, as might be expected, particularly successful. That the hopes of the ardent educationists of the democratic epoch will ever be fulfilled seems extremely doubtful. Great men cannot be made to order by any system of training, however perfect. *The most that we can hope to do is to train every individual to realize all his potentialities and become completely himself.* But the self of one individual will be Shakespeare's self, the self of another Flecknoe's. The prevailing systems of education not only fail to turn Flecknoes into Shakespeares (no system of education will ever do that); they fail to make the best of the Flecknoes. Flecknoe is not given a chance to become even himself. Congenitally a sub-man, he is condemned by education to spend his life as a sub-sub-man.[1] [My italics.]

The ordinary man, whether European or African, is neither a Flecknoe nor a Shakespeare, but, as we have been trying to show in the foregoing chapters, if he is encouraged to 'become completely himself' he has his own individual contribution to make to the life of the whole. This can only be achieved by recognizing differences and encouraging variety, and it is particularly important that Africans should understand this. One of the really complicating factors of the whole problem facing any European who sincerely wishes to explore and discover the specific individual needs of African children and how these can best be met, is that many Africans with some education, whether teachers or not, have it fixed in their minds that to be 'different' must mean to be 'inferior'. They try, therefore, by all the means in their power to give the impression that African children are no different from European children. Should a European indicate that he thinks African children are, in some respects, profoundly different from European children, this is all too often interpreted to mean something profoundly anti-African. The statement may have been intended as a heart-felt compliment on the one hand, and on the

[1] Aldous Huxley, *Proper Studies*, Essay on Education, London, 1929, p. 98.

other hand as the expression of a genuine desire to understand these differences, in order that the African child may be helped to develop along robustly independent lines, instead of being subjected to imposed European techniques which may be most unsuited and even harmful to him. This is in part due once more to the isolation suffered by many Africans, which renders it rarely possible for them to make comparisons, and colours their whole *Weltanschauung*. They do not know, for instance, that if you told a Frenchman he was 'just like an Englishman' the former would probably feel indignant, and in some cases grossly insulted. Neither can he appreciate that in French boys' schools *tu es Bosche* is a term of abuse. If you say a Frenchman is different from an Englishman no-one would attack you for being anti-French, even though the Frenchman is also a European. But if you state the still more obvious truth that an African is different from an Englishman you are in danger of being regarded as an anti-African menace. This is partly due, of course, to the fact that the African uses the word 'European' as a synonym for 'English'. It is also in large part due to the undiscriminating English sentimentalists who pander to this erroneous concept by supporting it wherever possible, in the belief that this is soothing to race relationships whereas it merely makes confusion worse confounded. I have heard English (that is European) teachers say things like, 'Oh, Nabongo reminds me of Jimmy Wilson' or, 'This class is just like one I taught at Harrogate'. Both statements require further investigation, but they are accepted with delight at their face value by the African teacher to whom they are often propitiatingly made, and who does not realize their more sinister implications. It needs to be emphasized in training college courses that the greater the intelligence, the greater is the ability to distinguish between ever-increasingly fine shades of differences. Even the least intelligent can see the 'sameness' of things, often where they do not exist, but to be able to detect subtle differences between things bearing superficial, or more than superficial, resemblances to each other, betrays an intelligence of a different order. Along with this recognition, the desirable emotional attitude should be fostered, namely the respect for these differences, precisely because such a respect embodies the 'reverence for life' which is the hallmark of those who consider human beings as ends in themselves and not as means to ends. (The leopard-skin, the symbol of 'the beautiful variety of things', is the indication of the spiritual freedom of man and a people.) What needs to be taught is that there are many different kinds of imagination, and many different kinds of intelligence; that a civilized society is a society of complements and all are needed to make up the pattern of the whole. This needs to be consciously taught, not merely by implication, because this individualistic mode of thinking and approach is fundamentally opposed to that on which the preservation of a tribal society depends. As this tribal society breaks down, one of the most poignant needs of Africans is for compassionate understanding of his insecurity, to help him to make a satisfactory psychological and spiritual adjustment to his unfolding future.

An objective attitude is often conceived as opposed to a mystic or magic attitude. The latter has been described as a characteristic of primitive man. The world of the primitive because of his magic mind, is dominated by the categories of identity and community; hence his mechanisms of adjustment are collective. The world of the primitive is not individualized, for both his physical and social environment is seen by him in the perspective of the whole.

. . . From the analysis of the primitive's behaviour one cannot easily conclude that he possesses the feeling of the specific character of his personality, or that the various situations in which he may find himself have their own specific character. His reactions are guided by collective formulas and are directed not so much towards the specific character of the situation as towards a general factor lying behind the things and the events of his world. Any act of adjustment to the primitive's world requires the individual's identification with his group. This type of adjustment, characteristic of the super-ego, is quite opposite to that produced by the ego. The former leads, sooner or later, to *Gleichschaltung* and communion, to the annihilation of the individual character of things and persons. The latter creates formal relations, it preserves and increases the individual character of things and persons, it is this world, based on the individual character of things and persons, that form the framework of a democratic way of life.[1]

(6) It would seem desirable that there should be somewhere in Uganda room for experiment outside Government or other control, where teachers should have the freedom and opportunity to investigate the problems which have been the subject of the foregoing chapters. Out of such an investigation, methods could evolve which would be based on the needs of the human beings in whose interests the investigations are taking place. Variety within the educational system must be permitted and encouraged.

On October 9th, 1962, Uganda celebrated her independence. Inevitably there will be a further increase in mass instruction and the application of mass techniques. There is a corresponding urgency to draw attention to the need for a liberal approach in teacher training; the need for a passionate appeal for encouragement of the life of the spirit, of all that is imaginative and creative in young Africans and their teachers.

I once attended an English course for teachers, held in Kampala, where a European education official made the following pronouncement: 'You should not allow the children to use their imagination until they have control of the language.' This would be funny if it were not tragic. As long as such attitudes dominate the African educational field, African childhood, youth and adulthood will remain in spiritual chains, and generations of African children will wait behind the glass, darkly, for the day when they can say with Helen Keller: 'Thus I came out of Egypt and stood before Sinai, and a power divine touched my spirit and gave it sight so that I beheld many wonders. And from the sacred mountain I heard a voice which said, "Knowledge is love and light and vision".'[2]

[1] Barbu, *Democracy and Dictatorship*, p. 79 (1956).

[2] Helen Keller, *The Story of My Life* (1947).

Teachers and teacher-trainers bear a heavy responsibility. 'I came that ye should have life and have it abundantly.' We should beware lest being required to han[illegible]n a little of the manna of this our heritage and our abundance we hand on instead—a pebble.

1 (*a*) NTATE

(*b*) SERUYINDA

2 MUTEBI

3 MUTEBI

4 GEORGE ZIWA

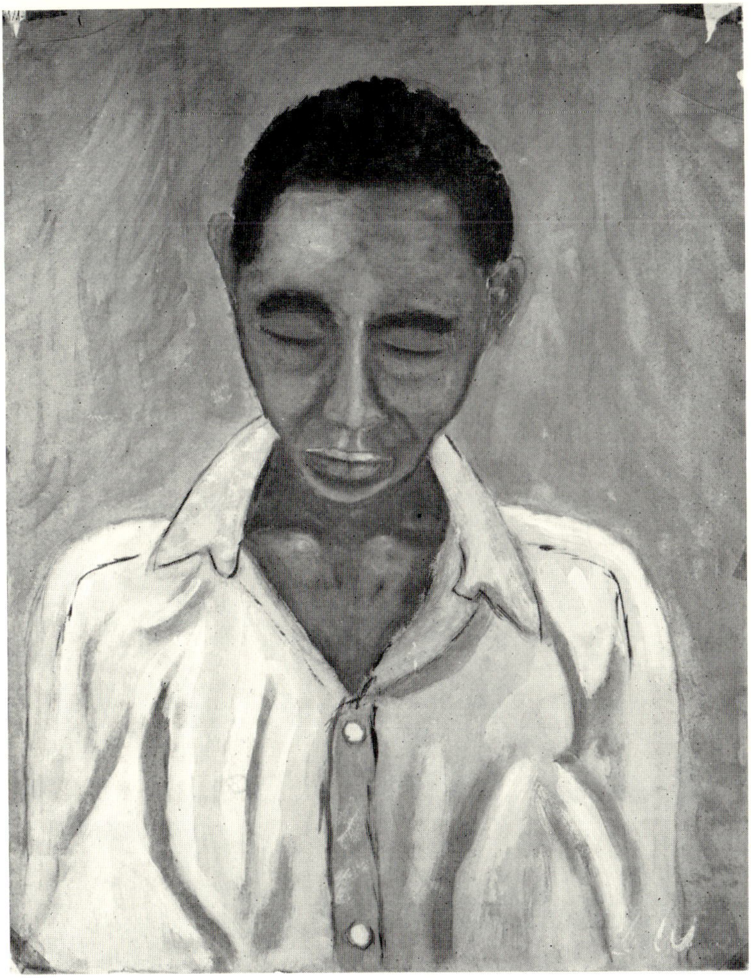

5 GEORGE ZIWA

6 KIRONDE

7 KIRONDE

8 (*a*) KIREMERWA

(*b*) SERUYINDA